Praise for *Innovating Lean Six Sigma*

A book that is both strategic and practical, *Innovating Lean Six Sigma* should top the reading list for anyone who wants to successfully implement operational excellence. The methods described in this book will drive significant financial value for your company, engage and develop your employees, and help you meet the ever-changing needs of your customers. Kimberly and Kristine have continued to build on the foundations of everything that we started, advancing the approach based on their work with clients from around the world, and have summarized their learnings in this easy-to-read book.

> —Michael L. George, bestselling author of *Lean Six Sigma* and *Lean Six Sigma for Services*

Our company implemented Lean Six Sigma after a period of rapid growth to become more process-focused, customer-focused, and data driven. The approach engaged and inspired our employees to improve our business processes, and we achieved a 10X ROI in the first year. Full of case studies and practical examples from the authors' many years of experience, *Innovating Lean Six Sigma* should top the reading list of any business leader.

> —Tom Wise, CEO, Superior HealthPlan

The Lean Six Sigma initiative at Dr Pepper Snapple has been a major contributor to its success since 2011. In that time, their free cash flow has increased to an all-time high and the stock price has more than doubled, outpacing its peers by nearly 100 percent. Dr Pepper Snapple is now the Consumer Products leader in both inventory and capital productivity and has publicly reported over $200 million in cash savings, all thanks to LSS. I was very blessed to establish and lead that initiative from 2011 to 2015 with the help of fantastic practitioners such as Kimberly Watson-Hemphill, who with this book has provided a terrific framework for any executive looking to achieve breakthrough results from Lean Six Sigma.

—Will McDade, Chief Financial Officer, Interstate Batteries, former Senior Vice President, Dr. Pepper Snapple

Innovating Lean Six Sigma is an executive's how-to guide for deploying and maintaining a successful process improvement initiative. The practical and insightful material has been indispensable in developing a framework and system to equip and engage our employees to improve the member experience by creating standardized, consistent, and value-added processes.

—Michael Crowl, VP Finance/CFO, University Federal Credit Union

The Lean Six Sigma principles described in the book have benefitted our business and have resulted in reducing our manufacturing times by over 50 percent, which allowed us to almost double our output! This was accomplished by performing simple line balancing, continuous flow, and using a takt rate board to monitor progress. We used these tools to balance the workload to allow for smoother flow and less downtime waiting on the next machine.

—Clint Lundquist, Continuous Improvement Leader, Everi

INNOVATING LEAN SIX SIGMA

A Strategic Guide to Deploying the World's Most Effective Business Improvement Process

Kimberly Watson-Hemphill
AND Kristine Nissen Bradley

New York Chicago San Francisco Athens London Madrid
Mexico City Milan New Delhi Singapore Sydney Toronto

1 2 3 4 5 6 7 8 9 0 DOC/DOC 1 2 1 0 9 8 7 6

ISBN: 978-1-259-58440-4
MHID: 1-259-58440-2

e-ISBN: 978-1-259-58441-1
e-MHID: 1-259-58441-1

Library of Congress Cataloging-in-Publication Data

Watson-Hemphill, Kimberly, author.
    Innovating lean six sigma : a strategic guide to deploying the world's most effective business improvement process / Kimberly Watson-Hemphill.
        pages cm
    ISBN 978-1-259-58440-4 (alk. paper) — ISBN 1-259-58440-2 (alk. paper)
    1. Total quality management.   2. Benchmarking (Management)
3. Six sigma (Quality control standard)   4. Quality control—Management.   I. Title.
    HD62.15.W384 2016
    658.4'013—dc23

                                                                2015032223

McGraw-Hill Education books are available at special quantity discounts to use as premiums and sales promotions, or for use in corporate training programs. To contact a representative, please visit the Contact Us page at www.mhprofessional.com.

Contents

Acknowledgments

We would like to thank everyone on the team at Firefly Consulting for their hard work and commitment to excellence for our clients. It is from our shared journey that we have learned how to innovate Lean Six Sigma to empower employees and drive results, a journey that has also been a personally fulfilling and rewarding endeavor.

A special thank you to everyone who helped with this book, in particular Jeff Kahne, Lisa Custer, Chuck Cox, Mark Sidote, Randy Boyd, Robert Watson-Hemphill, Julaine Calhoun, Heather Rafferty, Mike Hemphill, Sue Reynard, and Knox Huston.

Additionally, Kimberly and Kristine would like to thank their families for their encouragement and support.

Introduction

The Tao of Lean Six Sigma

The combined discipline of Lean Six Sigma has been around for well over a decade, and its component disciplines date back much further—a long enough time span to produce hundreds of deployments: some successful, some not.

If you look at the successful uses of Lean Six Sigma, you'll see a wide range of reported approaches and benefits. Some global corporations launched massive efforts to establish a now well-entrenched infrastructure that has generated millions or even billions of dollars in saved operating costs. Other companies started with small, localized efforts that expanded over time, ultimately leading to a cultural transformation. Century-old brand-name companies have brought in Lean Six Sigma experts to reinvigorate lagging business lines. High-tech companies have incorporated the design methodologies into their new product development operations to stay ahead of markets that can change overnight. Healthcare organizations have adopted Lean Six Sigma to ensure that patient focus is always given a top priority.

Even in the midst of the differences, however, there seems to be a common pattern of evolution among these organizations. Regardless of the shape, size, or application, what all the success stories have in common is that the business leaders managed to navigate their way through some critical questions and unite many different pieces of a complex puzzle into a coherent whole.

These leaders understood that in the Tao of Lean Six Sigma, there is no single right path. They became successful by defining what they wanted to achieve, creating a solid foundation, and then expanding where they used the methods and what tools they incorporated to meet their organization's needs. They didn't have to be perfect right out of the gate; instead, they focused on ways to continually learn from and leverage their lessons and gains. Also, these methods have evolved over time. Leading companies have learned to innovate, expanding the methods as well as their applications.

Thinking about Lean Six Sigma as a path instead of a destination can help you better understand how to launch a new deployment, identify ways to help a struggling initiative, and target the next steps to build on your foundation. Each of these aspects is addressed in this book:

- If you are just starting out and want to know how to shape a solid deployment, or if you have an existing program that isn't quite firing on all cylinders, then *Part 1* is for you. The first chapter gives an overview of the biggest questions that shape the decisions about the path you want to create. Other chapters address how to use metrics to help manage an improvement effort, how to get leaders more involved in championing a deployment, the importance of using assessments to drive effective project selection, and how to begin shaping a culture that is more supportive of Lean Six Sigma methods. The final chapter discusses a more formalized way to evaluate where you currently are in your Lean Six Sigma journey and how to identify reasonable next steps.

- *Part 2* is for companies that are well on the way to having a solid foundation and want to do more—tackle bigger problems, use more sophisticated methodologies, push the culture of improvement deeper into their company, and so on. The first chapter discusses business process management (BPM) and the important role it can play in ensuring high-level performance in core processes. Other chapters address design and innovation methods and their advantages when you are inventing new processes or products, the application of advanced statistical tools to tackle complex problems, setting up systems to better link strategy and execution, and how to tackle business challenges quickly with enterprise kaizen.
- We've also included a special chapter on the use of Lean Six Sigma in the *healthcare* industry because the need is so great and the demand so high.

We want to point out that this book is *not* about the specific tools and principles of the Lean Six Sigma methodology. You can learn about those mechanics from countless other resources. The focus in this book is on helping people think about ways to improve how they use Lean Six Sigma to drive business results. Don't settle for less from your own deployment or avoid a promising opportunity to engage employees and generate significant financial returns for your business. With this book, we hope to provide you with practical advice that will help you decide what to do next, no matter where you are in your improvement journey. You too can innovate your own Lean Six Sigma journey, and join the leading companies that are doing it right.

Part 1

Firing on All Cylinders

Building a Strong Foundation for a High-Functioning Lean Six Sigma Initiative

1

What's First?

The Big Four Questions
That Shape a Deployment

The headlines around Lean Six Sigma almost always involve big deployments that have been spectacularly successful: Caterpillar's 2001 Annual Report, for example, noted that in the first year of deployment, its gains from Six Sigma were already more than twice the implementation costs. By its 2002 Annual Report, Caterpillar was reporting net free cash flow of $645 million in its machinery and engine operations, attributed to Six Sigma. Eli Lilly and Company reported, "We exceeded our goal of $250 million in benefit from Six Sigma in 2006, and that is on track to double in 2007." The company's success continues. In its 2014 annual report, Eli Lilly reported 1,700 projects completed with financial benefits of $770 million.

Sounds pretty good, right? These were both great rollouts, continue to drive significant value, and are certainly the kinds of results that any executive would be happy to report to senior leadership, the board, or shareholders. And they set the standard for what other companies hope to achieve with their initiatives.

Based on these famous success stories, people may think that if they are to achieve meaningful results, they need to launch a large corporatewide deployment that requires an enormous investment of time and resources.

In reality, success with Lean Six Sigma has come in many shapes and forms. What the famous and the not-so-famous success stories have in common are not the goals, scale, or structure of the deployment; rather, it is that their leaders have thought carefully about how to bring together the specific pieces of the puzzle needed to build a foundation that works for them.

There are hundreds of decisions that go into building the foundation for a strong Lean Six Sigma program. The most important ones fall into the Big Four categories—basic and seemingly simple questions whose answers define the framework for a deployment:

- Why?
- What?
- How?
- Who?

Making sure you are clear about the answers to these questions will help you design or improve a Lean Six Sigma initiative. In this chapter, we'll walk through each question and discuss the different ways in which it can be answered. Our goal is to help people who are just starting out understand the cornerstones of success that they need to establish, and help those who are struggling with their deployments to understand what gaps they may need to address. (If your company already has clear answers to these questions, you may benefit from a more formal, structured assessment, which we'll discuss in Chapter 6.)

BIG QUESTION 1: WHY?

Although all of the Big Four questions are interrelated, the biggest impact comes from the question of *why* you are implementing Lean Six Sigma. If you aren't clear about the why, your decisions about who, what, and how are likely to miss the mark. As obvious as this sounds, too many companies fail to think through the *why* question in depth; their leaders hear about the big gains and the substantial dollars from the famous deployments and want a piece of that action—and that's as far as they go. Their *why* is couched only in terms of a certain figure on the bottom line.

It's true that for-profit, publicly held businesses need to be able to quantify the financial benefits from Lean Six Sigma fairly easily and have those benefits come fairly quickly, or else leadership loses interest. (And history has shown that, over time, successful deployments generate at least a 10 times return on investment.) But gains can almost always be measured in terms other than dollars, and the nonfinancial gains often provide an equally compelling answer to *why do this.* Here are three examples that illustrate different ways in which the *why* question has been answered:

● A financial services company had grown rapidly through acquisition and needed a methodology to unify the culture and streamline its core processes. Lean Six Sigma provided a foundation and methodology that established a common language concerning process improvement and product design. It also helped the company create a culture of continuous improvement. By using Lean Six Sigma to remove waste, the company was able to decouple its cost curve from its growth curve—meaning that it could generate much more value for the amount of effort invested, significantly increasing profitability.

- A manufacturing company was experiencing significant margin pressure as a result of overseas competition. The leadership team chose to deploy Lean Six Sigma to reduce operational expenses and leveraged the design methodologies to enhance the customer's experience and introduce new products. They also were able to use Lean Six Sigma to increase the skill level of the workforce and prepare people for future leadership positions within the company.
- A large hospital was interested in improving its patient satisfaction scores. Using Lean Six Sigma, the employees focused their improvement efforts on patient-facing processes that historically had caused patient frustration and dissatisfaction. The initiative was driven not by a need to reduce costs, but by a desire to better satisfy the hospital's customers. Ratings for the hospital improved in every category by 20 to 40 percent.

The *whys* in these three examples—aligning the culture, becoming more competitive, and increasing customer satisfaction—are common reasons for using Lean Six Sigma, but they represent just the tip of the iceberg. Your organization will have to define your own *why*. What would have to happen for your initiative to be considered a success? Ideally, think beyond the dollars to describe ways in which Lean Six Sigma can help you solve your organization's challenges. Perhaps a new market is opening up, the competition has made advances in services or technologies, or your company has to stem the loss of market share.

Being clear about the *why* will provide a compelling reason for using Lean Six Sigma and will shape the goals you set. It will also help you define what success looks like. If you're using Lean Six Sigma to become competitive in new markets, then success would be increased revenue and expanded market share. If you need to make operational improvements, then success could be measured in terms of reduced cycle times, lower costs, and/or higher quality.

BIG QUESTION 2: WHAT?

The *what* question for a Lean Six Sigma initiative means what problems and improvement opportunities will be addressed. Answering that question should start with defining what it is that you need to do substantially differently from and/or better than before in order to meet the challenge spelled out by the *why*. Do you need to be able to get product out the door faster in order to stay competitive? Answer more customer requests correctly to improve satisfaction? Reduce costs or improve quality to improve the bottom line? Create innovative products and services so that you can enter new markets? Unite your culture so that you improve communication and productivity?

Once you know broadly what issues you need to tackle, you can get more specific about choosing projects that will contribute to those goals. This is a linkage that has often not been handled well in the past. Decades ago, in the very early years of the quality improvement movement in the United States, teams were often allowed to select their own projects based on any criteria they wanted, including the convenience of the project leader. New deployments today sometimes repeat this mistake—in their eagerness to get the initiative going, the company lets individuals select any area from their daily job where they see an opportunity for improvement. At best, opportunities identified this way result in localized improvement. At worst, they lead to projects that have little impact on business results and that can quickly become a joke across the company. If management does not see the projects chosen as critical, support for the effort is likely to fade quickly.

As a reaction to this bottom-up approach, the pendulum then swung rapidly toward a top-down method: the people at the top of the business unit or organization would identify priority goals, which were then divided up and launched as projects. While projects must be linked to business priorities, a purely top-down approach, if not deployed correctly, can lead to massive, poorly scoped projects that can take years to complete.

To combat these problems, successful deployments today are based on structured project selection approaches that balance out competing factors so that projects have direct links to strategic goals (the *why* you have already identified), but also are meaningful to the frontline staff members who will do the project work. If this is an area where your company needs help, you'll find specifics about project identification and selection methods in Chapter 5. As a quick overview, the factors that go into the most robust processes incorporate:

- Both top-down and bottom-up methods for identifying potential projects
- Identification of diverse criteria for both benefit and effort that can be used to score the projects against the business priorities
- A prioritization process that evaluates each project against the weighted criteria

As you can probably predict, the focus of the project identification process will vary by organization. Here are two examples illustrating key differences:

- To identify the highest-value projects for its Lean Six Sigma rollout, a multinational manufacturer conducted a series of assessments at multiple plants, in the supply chain operations, in the sales organization, and in the regulatory functions. They tied their project selection and measurements to established operational targets involving revenue generation, quality, cost, and productivity. Looking across multiple areas for ideas that met the criteria led to a diversity of projects. For example, high-value opportunities were identified in improving plant efficiencies, streamlining the human resource process, reducing days' sales outstanding, and optimizing the sales process.

- A healthcare company began by identifying their core processes. They then linked their annual goals to improvement needs in those core processes as a way to select target project opportunities. Some projects directly improved patient care. Others improved satisfaction with the call centers. Some streamlined bureaucratic processes that delayed payment to all parties. Still others reduced costs, such as the cost of expired materials and obsolete medical supplies.

BIG QUESTION 3: HOW?

Many problems with the *how* of Lean Six Sigma are related to that old saying, "If you have a hammer, every problem looks like a nail." There is a wide variety of methods and tools that are included under the Lean Six Sigma umbrella, and in the past, many companies took the approach of applying the full set of standard tools to every problem. They would launch a Six Sigma investigation that lasted several months to solve a problem that had an obvious solution. Or they would apply a process improvement road map to a situation where a complete redesign was needed.

Six Sigma and Lean are both adaptable improvement approaches, but neither is suited to all problems under all circumstances. Likewise, there are different road maps that lead to different types of outcomes (improving existing processes or products versus developing new designs, for example).

Knowledge about when to use which method and which road map is more sophisticated today, and organizations that fail to take the differences into account can waste time and effort. The principles we recommend are:

- Develop expertise in both the Lean and Six Sigma methodologies so that you understand which toolset is appropriate when. A few people still hold out for a pure Lean or a pure Six Sigma approach, but they are in the minority.
- Use the DMAIC (Define–Measure–Analyze–Improve–Control) structure as the road map for problem solving and process improvement. There are two basic types of DMAIC projects:
  - The traditional Lean Six Sigma project team approach, where a group meets regularly over a period of time to solve a difficult problem that has no obvious solution. The emphasis is typically on tools that focus on understanding the voice of the customer, collecting the right data, and analyzing the data with statistical methods to identify the true root cause of the problem.
  - Kaizen projects, where a group of selected team members are brought together for an intense one-week period to complete a cycle of rapid improvement on a problem with a smaller scope. This structure is best used in situations where process waste or inefficiencies are a problem and the Lean toolset is more appropriate.
- Use the DMEDI (Define–Measure–Explore–Develop–Implement) road map for situations in which you need to design or substantially redesign a product, service, or process.

The emphasis in DMEDI is on understanding customer needs, creatively innovating and exploring design alternatives, and optimizing the design.

- Consider using business process management (BPM) to establish a solid foundation of knowledge about the needs and functions of core processes. BPM emphasizes measurement, documentation, and control. (See Chapter 8 for a discussion of BPM.)

BIG QUESTION 4: WHO?

Having staff members who are dedicated to continuous improvement was an innovation that arose when it became clear that it was unrealistic to expect people to run improvement projects and fulfill all of their regular job duties as well. Today, every organization that is successful with Lean Six Sigma has people who are dedicated either full- or part-time to project work, known by labels that are now part of the business lexicon (deployment champion, Black Belt, Master Black Belt, Green Belt, etc.). But there are still vast differences in the people that companies get to fill these positions and how much of their time is officially allocated to improvement work.

Back when the practice of using dedicated resources started, there were two common pitfalls in staffing these positions. Because there is a strong data element at the core of both Lean and Six Sigma, some companies picked their most technical colleagues. While this had the advantage that the people were able to learn the new tools easily, these more technically oriented staff members occasionally showed a tendency to become more enamored with the tools and data analysis than with the results or teamwork. Other companies simply assigned whoever was most readily available—perhaps because they were unsure about the potential of the effort and were therefore unwilling to devote their brightest or most promising colleagues. Companies that used people who, to put it politely, weren't wanted for any other position had difficulty generating the kinds of results that would build enthusiasm and support.

What practitioners came to realize was that it was much easier to teach people the tools and methodologies of Lean Six Sigma than it was to teach them leadership and teamwork skills. It was also clear that for a Lean Six Sigma initiative to be taken seriously, companies had to fill key positions—the deployment champions, Black Belts, and Master Black Belts—with top talent who were seen as having a bright future in the organization. Talented people who want to rise in the organization will want to make sure that they tackle important issues that will capture the attention of senior leaders. They will also want to make sure that they are using the methods that will give them the best possible chances of success. To make sure that these top people are successful during their Lean Six Sigma rotation, the best practice is for them to become full-time, dedicated Black Belts for a period of a year or two so that they have plenty of capacity to devote to improvement work.

Other lessons involving the *who* of Lean Six Sigma have come from deployments that simply failed to establish a foothold in the organization. This happened when the organization failed to link the Lean Six Sigma effort with the needs of the people who had the responsibility for running the business. All deployments, no matter what their size, take effort and commitment if they are to become established and to be sustained over time. That kind of dedication will happen only if supervisors, managers, and executives see the effort as key to *their* success and that of *their* part of the business. In short, the deployment must contribute to the business goals of line management. And the best way to make sure that this happens is to give line management oversight responsibility: have a C-level

Where What Meets Who

The *what* and *who* questions come together at this point because you have to think about how to best prepare the people involved in the deployment for their new responsibilities. The following guidelines are widely used today:

- Provide at least an awareness level of training to the executives and managers who will be sponsoring or providing oversight for the projects. Do the same for people who may be called upon to help out with the project work.
- Project leaders need an in-depth knowledge of the new methods. They will also need coaching on their projects by experienced practitioners as they learn to apply the new tools.
- Select a training curriculum that is appropriate for your business and the methodologies you will be using.
  - Services-based for transactional or service environments.
  - Operations-based for manufacturing or logistics audiences.
  - Healthcare is an unusual mix of manufacturing and transactional concepts, so training facilitated by practitioners with healthcare experience is recommended.

executive who champions the deployment and middle managers who actively participate as sponsors.

Organizations that follow these guidelines have reaped a secondary benefit: the experience with Lean Six Sigma has helped their managers and managerial candidates become better and more capable leaders. Here are three examples:

- A large hotel chain trained their manager candidates in Lean Six Sigma methods to ensure that future leaders were more data-driven, process-driven, and customer-focused.
- A pharmaceutical company wanted to broaden the skills of its high-potential employees and better enable them to work cross-functionally across the business. Lean Six Sigma gave them a new toolkit, and also provided opportunities for professional development.
- A financial services company that was experiencing rapid expansion needed to develop more of a process focus to keep up with its growth. The CEO selected Lean Six Sigma to develop a foundation of greater analytic abilities and data-based decision making within his management team.

BIG FOUR QUESTION ALIGNMENT

Working through all these questions, either at the beginning of a new deployment or when the deployment team is looking to make changes in an existing program, establishes a solid foundation for success, especially if you make sure of the links between all the elements.

As an example of how the questions come together, consider a consumer packaged goods company that was looking to enter new markets to expand their global reach and increase sales (see Figure 1.1). The company's leaders knew that there had been supply chain issues with similar expansions in the past, so they decided to implement Lean Six Sigma in key geographies throughout the supply chain to improve efficiencies, streamline operations, and reduce errors. Additionally, the new markets would require some completely new products as well as some minor product line extensions.

The company chose to pilot Design for Lean Six Sigma on the most critical of the new products, the ones that would require gathering significant new voice of the customer information. Because the expansion was critical to corporate strategy, the company assigned a team of dedicated, high-performing, full-time Black Belts to lead the projects. Additionally, the leaders were involved to ensure that the Black Belts would have the resources and support they needed.

FIGURE **1.1** Big Four question alignment example

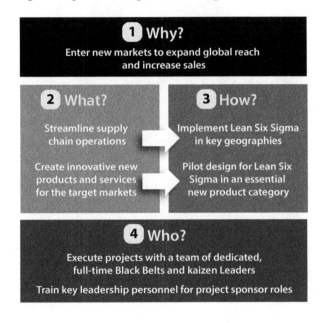

CREATING A VIRTUOUS CYCLE

A client CFO described it well when he once told us that the key decisions about a deployment can create either a virtuous or a vicious cycle, depending on how well they are handled.

If a company clearly ties the Lean Six Sigma initiative to a *why* that matters, then managers are more likely to devote highly capable people to the effort. Those people will have the ability to tackle important projects and will want to be taught the best methods for achieving their project goals, as this will help them personally be seen as successful by the rest of the organization. By producing good results, the company will achieve its goals, and everyone will view the effort as meaningful (see Figure 1.2).

FIGURE **1.2** Creating a virtuous cycle

On the other hand, when a company isn't clear about *why*, then managers won't know whether it's worthwhile to devote their most competent people to the program. They will be less likely to put much of their own effort into picking and monitoring projects or ensuring that standard best methods are used. Significant results will be harder to produce, and the deployment can quickly become marginalized.

The fact that these elements all influence one another is both good news and bad news. Since no initiative is going to get everything perfect the first time, how people handle challenges can set off an upward or downward spiral:

- If they probe into the causes of deployment problems, they can diagnose and strengthen the weakest elements, which will help them produce better results the next time around.

Suppose, for example, that the initial projects didn't produce the expected results, but the project leaders seem fully capable and engaged. The next time around, the project leaders should help improve the project selection process. Once the projects are perceived as being more meaningful and more likely to succeed, the company will have an easier time attracting top talent to fill the deployment positions and producing results that gain the attention of top management.

- The reverse is also true. If the deployment leaders fail to correct a problem, that can have a catastrophic impact on the other components. If a company with poor project results uses that as an excuse for managers to withdraw their support or for top talent to avoid getting involved, the results will get even worse and support will drop even lower.

As you surely know, a Lean Six Sigma initiative has a lot of moving pieces, and keeping all those pieces moving in sync is a challenge. Being clear about these basic questions—why, what, how, and who—can keep all the pieces aligned and help you avoid frustration. Successful deployments have a cohesive, integrated plan. Use your answers to these questions as a touchstone to make sure that everything is headed in the right direction.

2

Bolstering Leadership Support

WITH JEFF KAHNE, PhD

I don't know any other way to lead but by example.
—Don Shula, coach of the only perfect season in NFL history

Review the literature on leadership. Talk to experts. Talk to people in the trenches. Think about any corporate initiative you've been involved in. Every source will tell you that the single most important success factor for any major deployment is leadership support. That's why, no matter how well or how poorly your deployment is going, looking for ways to further engage and support the leaders is always going to be a step you should consider if you want to improve your results.

This work must involve both the leaders with line responsibilities, who must actively support the initiative if it is to contribute to significant business results, and those who are directly involved in shaping and running the Lean Six Sigma deployment (such as deployment champions). If you fail to support the line leaders, they will lose interest in the process; if you fail to support the deployment leaders, the effort will struggle. Either way, the result will be a deployment that fails to live up to its potential.

This chapter addresses three critical points of leadership involvement in a deployment:

1. Engaging business executives—the people whose budgets are at stake and who ultimately decide whether to invest in the deployment
2. Supporting sponsors—the line leaders who must allocate their own time and that of their resources to delivering the project work
3. Developing deployment leaders/champions—the people who are accountable for leading a successful program

Let's look at each of these leadership audiences in turn.

ENGAGING BUSINESS EXECUTIVES

A company with a large deployment was having difficulty gaining traction in the sales and marketing organization. In one-on-one meetings, the VP of sales and marketing seemed really positive about Lean Six Sigma. However, the deployment team didn't feel that he was doing anything to support the deployment. It also didn't seem like his enthusiasm was passed along to his direct reports.

After further conversations, it became clear that the VP wasn't sure what the deployment team needed from him to enable the deployment to be more successful. His direct reports had all heard about Lean Six Sigma, but they hadn't been given any specific direction on what was expected of them. Everyone called Lean Six Sigma "a good idea"—but they thought of it as something that was the job of the continuous improvement team, not something that needed their personal involvement.

This company's experience is typical of an odd phenomenon that we've run into many times in recent years. When we talk to deployment leaders, they complain to us that their business leaders aren't showing strong support. But when we talk to the business leaders, they say that they support these initiatives and are unaware of any specific actions that they should personally be taking.

Miscommunication or uncertainty about roles is common, so here's the challenge for you: Have you talked with your business leaders about what it is that you need from them if the deployment is to achieve its goals? Have you given them a job description of a supportive leader so that they understand the role they can play in strengthening the initiative? If the answer to either question is no, then that's one place to start in building stronger leadership support.

The sales and marketing unit of this Fortune 500 company took the following steps to align their leaders around clear roles and responsibilities:

- The Lean Six Sigma deployment team made a daylong presentation at a sales and marketing leadership meeting. During the session, the team members began with an introduction to Lean Six Sigma, followed by a discussion of sponsor and leadership roles and responsibilities. Then existing project teams from the business unit gave presentations describing several success stories, and the management sponsors of those projects shared their experiences. Participants got a clear message: imagine how great it would be if your area had results like these!

- Participants then got to work on their own project ideas. By the end of the day, each business leader had either a Master Black Belt or a Black Belt assigned to work with him or her. Each leader also identified one high-potential project from his or her area and was accountable for coming back in a month at the next leadership meeting with a completed charter for that project.

● Once those on the sales and marketing leadership team knew more about what was expected of them, and had seen success stories from their peers, they became much better partners in the process: they took a more active role in monitoring projects, making sure that their team had the necessary resources to complete the projects on time, shifting job responsibilities as necessary to remove roadblocks, and so on. They agreed to roll out sponsor training to the level below them in the organization and to spread the news about how management should be supporting Lean Six Sigma.

Conducting a Leadership Assessment

If you need to work with the leaders in any business area, our recommendation is that you start by talking with them to learn about their interests and concerns. This kind of assessment can be done at any point, but it can be even more helpful if it is initiated up front. The interviews should focus on five key areas (Figure 2.1).

The "leadership support" area is especially important because that will help you know which leaders you can rely on for their

FIGURE 2.1 Leadership assessment interview framework

support, which ones you'll have to convince (and the best way to convince them), and which leaders may be opposed. To learn about these areas, ask questions on topics such as:

- What has their previous experience been with change initiatives (both in your organization and in other organizations they have worked for)
  - What lessons they learned
  - What succeeded and what failed, and why
- What they've heard about the current Lean Six Sigma initiative
  - Why they think the company is going in this direction
  - Whether they agree with that reasoning
- What their attitude is toward the effort
  - Do they see ways in which Lean Six Sigma will help their unit or department, or do they view it more as a potential drain on resources?
  - How supportive are they?
- What they would like their role to be going forward

The answers to these questions will help you find out:

- Who is excited and who can't be bothered
- What concerns the leaders have
- Their fears based on previous initiatives
- What skills and attitudes you can draw on to make the initial work a success

The other four aspects of the interview will help you determine how to shape the initiative to best support your business. During this part of the interviews, you ask questions such as:

- Lean Six Sigma strategy
  - What are our key objectives?
  - What are our goals?

- Projects
  - Where should we start?
  - What would be your top priorities?
- Resources
  - How should we go about selecting resources?
  - Whom would you recommend?
- Culture
  - Is Lean Six Sigma a good fit with the culture?
  - Do you have any concerns?

Here is an example of how an initiative was shaped based on leadership interviews. A Fortune 500 company was planning to launch a Lean Six Sigma deployment across all functions and business units in the United States and Canada. There was a history of continuous improvement programs in the company's main manufacturing facility, including a limited Lean Six Sigma initiative. Before expanding the existing initiative, the company interviewed 60 leaders across the business and conducted five broader focus groups at major sites. In evaluating the insights gained from this process, the lessons were grouped into the five main dimensions of deployment effectiveness. Here are some of the insights that were gained:

- *Strategy.* The leaders thought the business case for the continuous improvement program should be presented in terms of profitability and growth. They did not want cost reduction to be the primary objective.
- *Leadership support.* Just over a third of the leaders (35 percent) considered themselves very positive about continuous improvement, and 55 percent were moderately positive. The remaining 10 percent either did not see a benefit or were not interested—they typically viewed previous initiatives as "flavor of the month" programs and categorized the new initiative the same way. The supportive

leaders were hopeful that, over time, the success of the program, along with positive influence from their peers, would change that negative impression. Middle management was concerned about the level of support that this initiative would receive from top management.

- *Projects.* The organization wanted tangible benefits and quick wins. Leaders also saw a considerable opportunity for improvement in the business and provided many specific ideas for projects that could be completed in a short time frame.
- *Resources.* Some of the executives were enthusiastic about staffing deployment leader and Black Belt roles with top talent: "If we can save $1 million per year by adding a $100,000 resource to lead projects, that should be a no-brainer." Others weren't as positive: "We have yet to find an idea that we don't like, and work-life balance is already a concern. This will just overburden us even more."
- *Culture.* In general, the culture was a good match— hard-working, lean-oriented, and empowered to make change. The leaders hoped that continuous improvement would build upon the positive aspects of the current culture and break down silos across business units.

Overall, the assessment provided the company with a deep understanding of its leaders' perspectives, which was used to tailor the deployment. For example, the company made sure to target first-round projects in the parts of the business that were run by the most enthusiastic leaders. Conversations about resources were started early on, which got leaders thinking about the need to allocate top talent to continuous improvement if they wanted to drive significant results. Messages consistently focused on profit and growth.

If your deployment is missing support at the middle levels and if your resources are constrained, then start by working with those managers who are most enthusiastic, and plan to expand the initiative later.

Helping Leaders Understand Their Role

Once you've completed a leadership assessment, the next step is to help the leaders understand their role. We recommend holding a kickoff event that has three parts:

1. The CEO or, at a minimum, the top executive for the work unit presents the goals, the case for change, and why the company is embarking upon Lean Six Sigma.
2. The Lean Six Sigma team provides awareness-level training on the methodology and presents an overview of the upcoming deployment.
3. The session closes by setting expectations for what is specifically required of the leadership team.

Afterwards, you should focus on those leaders who have demonstrated a natural affinity for continuous improvement and leverage their enthusiasm by helping them work on five areas:

1. *Creating a sense of urgency.* According to leadership expert John Kotter, not creating a "statement of urgency" is the root cause of 95 percent of large initiative failures. Leaders should develop a compelling message around what needs to happen in the organization, and define the consequences if the change doesn't take place soon, so that there is urgency concerning implementation. This is one of the most important actions that leaders often miss. They believe that just saying, "We are implementing Lean Six Sigma," is enough to mobilize the workforce. But that's far from true. For one thing, there is usually a time lag between when the C-suite sees a problem brewing and when the rank and

file believe it. You will have an easier time overcoming any potential initial resistance to Lean Six Sigma if the leaders are clear about why it has to happen now.

2. *Drive consistent messaging throughout the organization.* How the business leaders think and act concerning Lean Six Sigma will set the tone for everyone else. This is not a one-and-done thing—leaders can't refer to Lean Six Sigma once in a speech and never mention it again. They should take every chance to talk about the vision for how Lean Six Sigma can help the company (explaining the why) and each group's role in making its success a reality.

3. *Demonstrate the importance of Lean Six Sigma work.* Many of the problems that deployment leaders struggle with (projects with unimpressive results, staffing choices based on "who's available" instead of "who could do the work well") stem from a lack of demonstrated executive support. To avoid these issues, leaders should help establish objectives and goals that are linked to their priorities. Lean Six Sigma should be viewed as the way the leaders will achieve their priorities. If everyone knows that work on a Lean Six Sigma project will help drive an executive priority, people will pick important projects, devote adequate resources to the effort, and make sure that top-notch resources are assigned to projects.

4. *Review progress regularly.* Executives should review Lean Six Sigma deployment metrics and results at regular management meetings. Part of the review should include presentations of example projects by belts and the sponsors. This will give both the deployment and the individuals involved increased visibility and help build momentum for the program. By presenting both successful projects and also some that could have been done better, there is an opportunity for learning and improvement.

5. *Remove obstacles to success.* Lean Six Sigma efforts don't exist in a vacuum, separate from everything else that's happening in an organization. It's part of the responsibility of leaders who are committed to the effort to deal with the critical issues that could prevent the organization from using Lean Six Sigma to achieve its vision. They should be relentless in looking for and removing barriers to success (and this may include people).

Monitoring Leadership Engagement

As a deployment matures, it's important to keep on top of leadership engagement—and to be proactive if there are any signs that a leader's attention or energy is waning. There are many signs that will tell you just how engaged your leaders are in supporting Lean Six Sigma and whether they view it as a distraction or a business priority. Engaged, supportive leaders will:

- Establish goals and priorities based on annual business goals.
- Contribute to project selection.
- Help select top talent for continuous improvement efforts.
- Share project results in speeches, updates, and so on.
- Attend executive training.
- Participate in steering committees.
- Make sure that a review of Lean Six Sigma progress is a standard item on executive agendas.
- Publicly recognize both successes and the learning that comes from failures.
- Use continuous improvement techniques in their personal work.

If you don't see these things happening, then Lean Six Sigma isn't part of the DNA of the business, and you will need to work with the "lagging" leaders to find out why. Are they like the executive we mentioned earlier who just didn't know what his role should be? Are they struggling with challenges and need support from executives higher up?

Involving Leaders in Governance

One of the best ways to make sure that Lean Six Sigma efforts are tied to business priorities is to have the deployment overseen by an executive steering committee. This group can be a powerful coalition that supplements the role of the deployment champion (discussed later in this chapter), but the steering committee could also run the deployment itself under the right circumstances. Here's an example.

A healthcare organization was under considerable pressure to reduce costs, without any reduction in quality or patient care. Benchmarking results indicated that the organization's internal costs were high, and also that process improvement could be a significant opportunity.

An executive steering committee consisting of the CEO, COO, and CFO was formed to lead the direction of the Lean Six Sigma program. This committee and the deployment champion initially met every other week to get the program off to a good start. After that, the group met quarterly where they focused on confirming or redefining program goals, approving projects that were to be executed within that quarter, addressing issues, and breaking down roadblocks.

The executive steering committee also required project leaders to present periodic updates on their progress. This not only helped motivate the project leaders to pursue significant results, but also let the executives experience the enthusiasm that these people had for making improvements that mattered to the business.

This process also resulted in additional learning about the organization. For instance, one of the biggest issues that the steering committee identified was the lack of data availability. With high-level executive sponsorship, the deployment team was able to work with the IT organization to make the changes needed to improve data availability. This action had broad impact and improved the reporting of metrics across the organization.

Creating a coalition of leaders who are taking an interest in Lean Six Sigma can have a powerful impact on the organization. Here's another example.

An East Asian manufacturing facility that was part of a global company with headquarters in the United States had followed the company's directive to launch a Lean Six Sigma program. But the deployment was approached piecemeal, and only one department had made any headway. A leadership assessment (like that described earlier in this chapter) was conducted to evaluate the leaders' knowledge of and interest in Lean Six Sigma. The general manager discovered that there was a wide gap between the sense of urgency seen among some senior managers and the disinterest among the rank and file.

To close this gap and reenergize the initiative, the general manager created what he called the Process Council, which consisted of him and all of his direct reports. For the next six months or so, this council played the role of deployment champion. Its members reassessed the priorities and allocation of Lean Six Sigma resources and ended up shutting down some projects and launching others. They shifted resources to match the new priorities.

Eventually, the Process Council began handing over the management responsibilities to a deployment champion. But achieving widespread implementation would have been impossible had the leaders not demonstrated through their direct involvement that they were absolutely committed to using Lean Six Sigma to solve the plant's business challenges.

SUPPORTING SPONSORS

In many, many deployments, the executives are enthusiastic about the financial benefits that will come from Lean Six Sigma, the belts are excited about using new tools and methodologies on real-world problems—but meanwhile, middle management is often referred to as the "layer of clay" that resists organizational change. That's too bad because the role of project sponsors most often falls to midlevel managers whose primary responsibility involves the day-to-day management of operational or strategic areas. These manager-sponsors are a critical element connecting what is happening with the business and how the Lean Six Sigma deployment can help.

The lack of engagement of these sponsors often comes about because much of the focus in the Lean Six Sigma community is on the very top and bottom of the deployment ladder: how to get top executives engaged and making sure that the various belts get adequate training and coaching so that they can perform this new work. The middle levels are skipped over in terms of time and attention, which means that their fears and concerns may go unrecognized. Many managers are worried that it will make them look bad if a process in their area needs improvement, concerned about what is required of them in terms of time and resources, or even fearful of being stuck with solutions that they don't like. If these concerns and fears are never addressed, it's no wonder, really, that midlevel managers often turn skeptical and become obstacles to deployment progress. It usually doesn't take members of this group long to figure out that they have the most to lose if the status quo is disrupted. So when they are given the option of committing 20 percent of their energy to supporting the new initiative or 120 percent of their energy to proving that the new way won't work, some of them get busy on the proof.

If midlevel managers do not endorse and actively sponsor projects, you'll have a hard time producing results that are meaningful to the organization. It is very demoralizing for a team if they do not have the enthusiastic support of their sponsor. The worst sponsors don't make any time for the project, do not help the team overcome obstacles, do not support the team's ideas, and avoid ownership of the solution after it is implemented. When put forth this bluntly, it is obvious that it would be nearly impossible for a project with this type of sponsor to be successful.

Do You Have the Right Sponsors?

The project sponsor should be the person who "owns" the process that is being tackled in the proposed project. Typically, the sponsor is one level above the Black Belt in the organization. The very best sponsors are willing to:

- Make time to meet with the team leader on a regular basis to provide feedback and remove obstacles.
- Lead the gate reviews.
- Help with resource availability.
- Help with solution implementation.
- Attend sponsor training, or have even been through Belt training at some level (Black, Green, or Yellow), so that they have knowledge of the Lean Six Sigma process.

As time goes on, you can also help encourage sponsors by including them as part of the reward and recognition system put together to recognize teams and belts. For example, one company gives an annual "Sponsor of the Year" award.

In organizations with good alignment, the sponsors' annual goals are at least partially based on improving the metrics that their Lean Six Sigma team's projects are targeted to improve.

Teaching Sponsors About Their Role

As with senior leaders, a key contributor to the perceived lack of sponsor support is often that no one has educated the sponsors about their functions and responsibilities. A sponsor's job is to assist in the "care and feeding" of the project from beginning to end, from chartering to sustaining the gains. These responsibilities include:

- Identifying projects with meaningful business impact that align with business goals
- Writing the charter
- Assisting belts in scoping and staffing projects
- Helping to identify and recruit team members
- Monitoring projects and meeting with belts to review project progress
- Attending gate reviews with the belt, coach, and team
  - Providing a business perspective on project progress
  - Encouraging the belt and team to meet project goals and timelines
- Removing barriers
- Assisting with the implementation, if needed
- Being accountable for maintaining project gains

The best method of communicating this information is by developing a sponsor training course that not only educates the sponsors about Lean Six Sigma, but also generates tangible outcomes. That way, leaders begin trying on their sponsor hat by getting involved in identifying and selecting projects and drafting charters for one or two of their highest-priority project ideas. Though such work could in theory be done in one-on-one coaching sessions, a benefit of getting it started in a group training session is that you often get good interaction between sponsors, who come to a shared understanding of their role and the path forward for the deployment. A sample sponsor training agenda is provided in Figure 2.2.

The agenda incorporates several elements that are critical to creating effective sponsors. For one thing, the leaders will need a basic understanding of the Lean Six Sigma methodology (the first item on Day 1). We recommend enhancing their awareness and understanding via a fun and interactive simulation that will take them through the DMAIC phases and introduce the basic tools (the second item

FIGURE 2.2 Sample sponsor training agenda

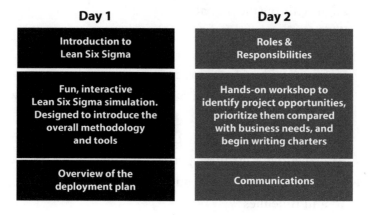

Day 1	Day 2
Introduction to Lean Six Sigma	Roles & Responsibilities
Fun, interactive Lean Six Sigma simulation. Designed to introduce the overall methodology and tools	Hands-on workshop to identify project opportunities, prioritize them compared with business needs, and begin writing charters
Overview of the deployment plan	Communications

on Day 1). The focus for the rest of the first day and the beginning of the second day then shifts to describing the deployment plan and helping participants understand what their role will be. The majority of the second day is spent making tangible progress on project identification and selection, with the participants working together to identify and prioritize opportunities and, as time allows, begin drafting charters. By the end of the training, the sponsors should have a good understanding of the methodology, the deployment plan, their role, and the projects that will be launched moving forward.

DEVELOPING DEPLOYMENT LEADERS

The counterpart to developing strong support from business-line leaders is doing the same for the people who are responsible for shaping and managing the deployment. Table 2.1 compares the characteristics we've seen in deployment leaders whose efforts have struggled with the characteristics of those who lead high-achieving deployments.

TABLE 2.1 Effective deployment leaders

	Marginal or underproducing deployments	High-achieving deployments
Typical champion	Black Belt or midlevel manager	Director or vice president
Reporting relationship	To department head	To a VP or, ideally, someone at the C-level
Reputation	Put in place because he or she had time	Well respected for his or her competence and past accomplishments
Attitude	Resigned	Enthusiastic
Background	May or may not be educated or experienced in Lean Six Sigma. Probably has little experience in leading change	A successful and capable change leader. Trained—or interested in dedicating the time to becoming trained—in Lean Six Sigma

High-performing deployments have top talent in the deployment champion role. The person's responsibilities include:

- Accountability for developing and hitting program metrics
- Providing deployment tactics in his or her area of responsibility (number of belts, projects, setting project goals)
- Driving project selection and prioritization; managing the project portfolio
- Actively promoting the program through communication of objectives and results
- Selecting candidates for key positions (Master Black Belt, Black Belts, Green Belts)
- Providing support for belts when required
- Interfacing with executives on strategy
- Being a force for creativity and innovation—pushing groups to examine any supposed limitations closely

Depending on the size of the deployment they are overseeing, the deployment champion may be full-time or part-time (but should be at least 25 percent dedicated). The most important quality of deployment champions is their ability to lead change.

Involved, Effective Leaders

In every deployment, there will be a range of support for the effort among your leadership. So one key tactic is to work with enthusiastic supporters to make sure they understand how to show their support (the actions they should take and the messages they must send).

Your job as an advocate of Lean Six Sigma is to think about what you can do to best support your leadership. The more you can do to shape the deployment to meet your leaders' business needs, communicate with them, and identify specific ways in which you can help them be successful, the more supportive and engaged they will be.

Making sure your leaders know how to support your effort and how you can support them is the best way to create a team of involved, effective leaders who will put in the effort and devote the necessary resources to make your deployment success a reality.

3

Got Culture?

With Jeff Kahne, PhD

We were on an initial conference call with the executive team of a prospective client, and we asked them to describe the company's culture. There was dead silence; we could even hear crickets chirping in the background. Silence is a common reaction when we ask people about their organization's culture. It isn't a question that companies often consider, let alone thoughtfully discuss. Culture runs below the surface of most organizations.

Obviously, the answer to the question, "Got culture?" is yes. Every group has its own culture. It is a natural outcome any time human beings associate with one another. Perhaps that's why so many organizations take their culture for granted.

To get the most out of your Lean Six Sigma efforts, you must be willing to critically examine your culture and decide whether it supports what you want to achieve or whether it is a barrier. Answering that question and addressing any disconnects can help drive sustainable, breakthrough improvements. Failing to ask that question or to fix the disconnects will put a ceiling on what you can achieve.

Cultural issues also come into play in companies that are dissatisfied with their current culture and want to reshape it. Companies do better in today's marketplace if they are innovative, responsive, and efficient—all qualities that are associated with the Lean Six Sigma discipline.

In this chapter, we look at those aspects of culture that support the success of Lean Six Sigma, and discuss concrete steps you can take to ensure alignment and foster values that support improvement. We also look at how Lean Six Sigma efforts can help you drive a more vibrant, competitive culture.

Values That Support Improvement

All improvement disciplines are based on a number of underlying principles, such as the importance of seeing your work through the customer's eyes, collecting data to pinpoint the causes of problems, and thinking scientifically about how to make changes that truly solve those problems.

While most of the typical organizational values (respect, integrity, and the like) support these principles, there are several that increase in importance when the goal is to use Lean Six Sigma to drive business results. These include:

- *We focus on customers.* From the prioritization of potential projects to decisions about what parts of a process are most important to get right, the Lean Six Sigma methodology requires knowledge of customer needs and requirements.
  If your company already does a good job of understanding your customers' perspectives, this will be a natural synergy. If it does not, then you can use the customer-centricity

techniques built into the methodology to benefit both your deployment and your organization as a whole.

- *We work to continually improve our processes.* The foundation of Lean Six Sigma is seeing work from a process perspective: as a series of steps linked by inputs and outputs, all of which can be documented, studied, and improved. Organizations that have a strong process orientation will find that Lean Six Sigma is perfectly consistent with their approach. Those that are not used to thinking in terms of processes may struggle at first to do the groundwork necessary for improvement, but in the long term, they will see significant benefits.

- *Data trumps opinion.* The Lean Six Sigma methodology uses data to calculate baseline performance at the beginning of the project, measure the amount of improvement at the end, and monitor the results. As with a process orientation, organizations that are naturally data-driven will have a relatively easy time meeting these requirements; those that run more on intuition will need to be especially vigilant in making sure that employees are taught (and use) the skills they need if they are to gather and interpret data. Either way, implementation of Lean Six Sigma establishes an expectation that data will be used to make decisions, an attitude that spreads beyond projects to the general running of the business.

- *Success requires teamwork.* A key to success with Lean Six Sigma projects is incorporating the contributions of people with different perspectives and expertise. Team members must *pool* their knowledge and skills to get the best results. Cultures that naturally value teamwork have an easier time with this aspect than those that reward lone ranger efforts.

While defining broad organizational values like these is a good start, it's also important to think about the values that the people responsible for the improvement efforts should have (and that the organization must learn to appreciate). They include:

- *Tenacity.* Leading change efforts and even individual projects can be difficult. People who already have a "stick with it" attitude will be able to push forward through the challenges.
- *Curiosity.* The Lean Six Sigma methodology is an exercise in detection, deduction, and investigation. People who naturally wonder why things are done a certain way and are always asking themselves how the work could be done better are likely to thrive in a Lean Six Sigma environment—and to pass that enthusiasm on to others.
- *Risk taking.* One truism is that improvement requires change. You can't get better results if you keep doing things the way you are doing them now. Success with Lean Six Sigma requires people who are willing to break with the status quo and risk suggesting improvements that could change the business for the better. To make these kinds of people successful, an organization needs to cultivate an environment that supports risk taking and change that is supported by data and evidence.

Without these organizational and personal values, Lean Six Sigma cannot work at maximum effectiveness or efficiency. If your organization already has established these values and acts in ways that are consistent with them, you're ahead of the curve. But we often encounter situations in which these improvement-supportive values run counter to the status quo. Reshaping a company's values is not easy, but the rewards in terms of improved outcomes are well worth the effort.

VALUES-BEHAVIOR ALIGNMENT

When values and behavior are aligned, you have a situation in which what is "important to me" is also "important to the organization," and is supported and rewarded through the organization's philosophy and culture (Figure 3.1). While you will probably never completely merge these three elements, the closer you get to the level of intrinsic motivation, the more the desire and willingness to go that extra mile will emerge.

FIGURE 3.1 Alignment of values and culture

This link between behaviors, values, and culture is a critical indicator of how successful you will be with Lean Six Sigma. Unfortunately, we see a lot of mismatches in the workplace between the values that are important to Lean Six Sigma and the actions taken by the organization. Some common examples are shown in Table 3.1.

When we find the kind of mismatches shown in Table 3.1, we see companies that will have additional challenges in achieving results with Lean Six Sigma.

TABLE 3.1 Mismatch of values and behaviors

What They Say	What They Do
"We value honesty"	Anyone who speaks the truth to the boss gets shut down, or people fear that telling the boss a hard truth will negatively affect their careers
"Everyone should work as a team"	Only individual achievement is acknowledged and rewarded. Achievement of goals is tracked for *individuals*, not for teams
"Quality is our goal"	Quality standards are allowed to slip when time or budgets are tight
"Innovation is key to our success"	Leadership stifles any idea that isn't 100 percent certain to work

For example, when it turned out that the executives on the conference call we mentioned earlier could not easily describe their company's culture, we asked them what values they thought were important in supporting their improvement initiative. They mentioned the things you'd expect to hear: treating people with respect, being honest, and focusing on the customer.

The best way to evaluate what values are truly in place, however, is to look at how people and companies behave. So we next asked the executives to describe the behaviors they saw that were related to these values. One admission they made was: *"People here want to be nice and polite. They won't say anything negative to your face, but they sure will once you've left the room."* While not a certain indicator of trouble, this statement was a warning sign that the behaviors that were common in this company might not be completely consistent with the value of "honesty." We'd have to watch to see whether people at this company would feel comfortable speaking up about problems, which is a key element in improvement projects.

In contrast, here are two examples of companies doing it right and seeing the results:

A Lean Six Sigma deployment in a pharmaceutical company was launched in part to drive a stronger focus on the customer. The deployment leaders knew that most of the employees had come onboard because they wanted to improve health outcomes for patients (customers), and so the deployment team developed messaging that linked Lean Six Sigma goals to that motivation. The leaders also knew that they would need to tailor specific Lean Six Sigma goals to the business goals for each major business area. For example:

- Employees in R&D heard that the effort had been launched to help reduce the development time for new medications in order to get lifesaving pharmaceutical products to patients more quickly. Projects were selected to support that goal, focused on driving metrics related to speed of development and quality of the new product pipeline.

- Employees in manufacturing heard that the goal of using Lean Six Sigma was to reduce costs and increase quality so that the company could provide patients with affordable, high-quality medications. Project selection and measurements were tied to established operational targets involving quality, cost, and productivity.

- With the values of the organization, the departments, and the Lean Six Sigma deployment aligned, the methodology was positioned for success within the organization's culture.

- In the Lean Six Sigma deployment of a financial services company, one value that became a priority was teamwork. All of the senior leaders made sure that they took notice of effective teamwork. For example, at the end of a seven-week project with a team that identified $180 million in hard and soft savings, a senior vice president took the whole team out for a nice dinner. He didn't just authorize a dinner expense. He didn't just congratulate the team leader. He took the whole team out for dinner, stayed the entire time, and talked with the people who had actually done the work. Most of the team members had never met this senior vice president before or spent time with anyone at his level in the organization. This simple dinner reinforced their positive feelings concerning the project. Everyone not only wanted to be involved with additional projects, but also spoke positively about the opportunity with coworkers who were considering getting involved.

These two examples show how behavior tied to values can support progress with Lean Six Sigma.

CREATING BETTER ALIGNMENT

A deployment leader or senior executive in charge of a deployment has a responsibility to look for misalignments between values and behaviors, and then work within her capacity to create better alignment. She may not be able to change the values embraced by the organization as a whole, but she can and should try to embrace the supportive values within her sphere of control.

The place to start is to examine the organization's values (which are probably found in a written values statement) and compare them to how the organization actually behaves (its operational philosophy): What policies does the organization have in place? Which of them does it enforce? Was a values statement communicated to employees? What does the organization reward and recognize? How do people actually behave in the workplace?

Pretend you are a brand-new employee coming to work at your organization. You see a sign on the wall that lists your company's values (probably including words such as *integrity*, *quality*, *teamwork*, and *continuous improvement*). As you begin to walk around the building, think about what observable behaviors you would expect to see if those values were actually being practiced. (Like watching TV with the sound turned down—you're looking not for what people are saying, but for what they are doing.) Once you have a list of behaviors in mind, go out and look for them in your workplace. Make a checksheet and tick off the number of times you actually see each behavior. Keep track. Which ones do you see? Are they sporadic or systemic?

Now ask other people to do the same thing and bring them into the discussion—what did they see? If any of you didn't see the behaviors you expected, what *did* you see? What do the behaviors you saw tell you about the real values that are at work in your organization?

Now comes the hard part: making an honest evaluation of whether your stated values and the observed behaviors are aligned. What does the evidence tell you about the *real* values in your organization? Your *real* operational philosophy? And, more important, are these values and philosophy consistent with what you want to achieve?

When doing this evaluation, you have to be critical. For example, does your operational philosophy truly inspire trust, teamwork, and continuous improvement? Or are you sending mixed messages— saying one thing, but doing another? For example, we've had companies say that they valued innovation and risk taking, but their policies required every new idea to be vetted by the legal department prior to any presentation, even to an internal audience.

Areas of misalignment should be targeted for action and follow-up, with the idea that the assessment should go full circle. When you know what values you want to reinforce, articulate the behaviors (of both the organization and the individual) you want to see that are consistent with those values. For example, if you say that trust is important, what do you mean by that? How would you know whether people trusted one another? How can you recognize and reward trust? Don't just define the *word* trust—define the behaviors associated with trust.

When you know what behaviors you want to see, make sure that the behaviors:

- Are supported by the senior leadership.
- Support your organization's goals and objectives, and are *not* in opposition to the organization's vision.
- Are understood by all team members.
- Are acknowledged and rewarded.

One piece of advice: you'll go crazy if you try to write down rules identifying everything that people *shouldn't* do. It's impossible to write rules that cover every situation. Even if there were hundreds of rules, there would still be times when people would have to decide what to do in situations that the rules don't cover. So it's far more effective to focus on the values that you want to demonstrate and a few key behaviors that are consistent with those values. Make sure that people understand what is important to the organization and how it applies to them.

The great organizational strength in this alignment comes when you are faced with something unknown or unpredictable. When you are faced with a situation with which you have no experience and for which there are no precedents, the odds of your making a wrong decision are reduced dramatically if your solution is congruent with the organization's values and your personal values, and is supported by the organization's operating philosophy.

The Ideal Three-Way Alignment

The best situation for an organization is when the two elements discussed here—*organizational values* and *operational philosophy*—are also aligned with the third critical element, people's *personal values*. That creates a positive reinforcement cycle: what is important to each individual is also important to the organization and will be rewarded through the operational philosophy.

You will never completely merge these three elements because people's personal values are largely shaped by the time they reach adulthood. But the closer you get through recruitment, alignment, and reinforcement, the more you will create a culture in which there is an intrinsic motivation, desire, and willingness to go that extra mile.

A Case Study in Culture Change

A plastics manufacturer that was trying to come out of bankruptcy acknowledged that it had a culture of command-and-control management. The unstated mantra was, "Do as I say." The company was turning to Lean Six Sigma to help it improve operationally, and the leaders realized that if the deployment was to work, they needed to create a new culture. They needed to emphasize inquiry and teamwork. They wanted to have managers ask, "What do you think?" more often and behave in ways that demonstrated, "We are in this together."

The employees wanted to believe that the new management team was serious about this, but they were not easily convinced. The starting point was to create better alignment from top to bottom.

Everyone was educated about the new vision for the company's future and why the old way of doing business was unsustainable given current market conditions.

More important, though, this message was backed up with leadership behaviors that demonstrated support—every single day. For example:

- The general manager attended every shift change meeting every day, and would ask what he could do to help that shift achieve its goals and become more effective.
- When behaviors didn't match values, the leaders took action to change those behaviors, up to and including termination for repeated violations.

Other changes were made as well. For example, to improve teamwork and collaboration, the production and maintenance departments created combined teams that were given more and more responsibility for production. These teams were trained not only on the tools of Lean Six Sigma, but also on the business and how the work of each team affected the business. Eventually, line maintenance and production associates could explain how their preventive maintenance procedures affected EBIDTA—not just parroting back what they'd been told, but explaining it in their own words.

With these kinds of changes, slowly the dictatorial "you do as I say" culture was replaced with high-performance work teams that understood how what they did on a day-to-day basis affected the company. And these cultural changes led to business results. Over a three-year period, the company went from bankruptcy to having customers ask, "What have you done? Your quality is so good now!" and "Can you come show us how to improve that much?"

If you've ever worked in an organization that was trying to change its values, you'll know that it's not easy. Getting people to value the improvement process and tools is difficult, and if there aren't simple steps they can take, they won't do it. Even in this manufacturing company, where the future was bleak at the outset, there were a number of things about the new culture that some people didn't like. As just one example, maintenance personnel had established the norm of taking their work breaks even if they were in the middle of fixing a production line that was down—which led to a lot of lost production hours. In the new mentality, getting the production line back up and running was the priority. Other people were uncomfortable with the new reliance on data, and still others with the emphasis on teamwork. In the end, some people opted out and chose to work somewhere else rather than change. However, on the whole, the cultural changes led to greater employee engagement, and the company experienced significant improvement.

SHAPING CULTURE WITH LEAN SIX SIGMA

The relationship between culture and Lean Six Sigma is a two-way street. Until now, we've focused on thinking about ways in which culture can support Lean Six Sigma, but the reverse is true as well. You can use your Lean Six Sigma efforts to help shape your organization's culture.

Obviously, one of the factors that is needed in order to shift your company's culture is to expose as many people as you can to the ideas through training and experience, and through the verbal and behavioral messages that the leaders send. You won't change a culture to be more improvement- and customer-oriented if only Black Belts understand the concepts and are trained in the skills. You need to have a plan that involves the whole organization in thinking and acting in new ways.

That said, don't rush to train everyone at once. People rarely become convinced of the value of Lean Six Sigma simply because they've attended an awareness or other training session. They need to apply the concepts and experience the benefits that come from a streamlined, more efficient, and more effective workplace. Your plan needs to be able to accommodate not only appropriate levels of training, but also the opportunity for people to participate on meaningful projects. For that reason, in some company cultures, an evolutionary model—perhaps cascading the effort down gradually or using a viral approach where you launch Lean Six Sigma in some areas, then let success in those areas drive interest in other areas—can be a more appropriate approach than a massive training effort.

The speed of the evolution will be determined by the resources you have and the urgency of your business priorities. There have been instances in which culture change happens quickly, but only when the reasons are clear, compelling, and undeniable. (Do you remember how quickly it became taboo to make jokes about airport safety after 9/11?)

For the most part, however, the kinds of culture changes associated with Lean Six Sigma take much longer. It's more like trying to turn an aircraft carrier than a Jet Ski. But just like turning an aircraft carrier, you can reach the goal if you are clear about your target and consistent in taking actions that are aligned with your intended results.

You can help reinforce this effort by being strategic about how you staff the Lean Six Sigma deployment positions and leverage their experiences, as we'll discuss next.

Stack the Deck Through Deployment Staff Selection

A chain of popular BBQ restaurants in Texas was one of the first restaurants ever to receive the prestigious Malcolm Baldrige National Quality Award. As a customer in its restaurants, it was easy to see the efficiency of the company's processes and its commitment to quality. At every opportunity, the CEO would emphasize the importance of selecting the right staff. He repeatedly said that he could teach someone everything that she needed to know about the restaurant business, but he could never teach people to smile and want to serve the customer.

Lean Six Sigma is similar. As we mentioned before, it's relatively easy to teach any smart person the technical skills and methodologies, but it's much more difficult to teach them the required people and leadership skills. You can't force someone to *want* to make the business better; he has to come by it naturally.

Every organization that launches a Lean Six Sigma effort has to make dozens, if not hundreds, of decisions about how to staff the deployment. We advise that, in addition to other criteria for core positions—deployment champions, Master Black Belts, and Black Belts—you think about ways to screen for behavioral characteristics that demonstrate the supportive values. That means, for example, that you may not want to choose someone who is a very strong individual performer, but who does not do as well with a team. Ideally, you want to pick people for the core positions who will be living examples of the values you want to encourage in the organization. These are usually the high-potential individuals that everyone wants for key roles in their department, team, or project work.

Use Improvement Experience to Groom Leadership Candidates

In today's markets, every organization needs to make sure that it is efficient and effective; most also want to be creative and innovative. So what skills do their managers and future leaders need? The very same skills that people get from going through Lean Six Sigma training and leading multiple improvement projects: analytical thinking, an improvement orientation, an understanding of creativity techniques, and so on. Furthermore, having people work on diverse Lean Six Sigma projects is a great testing ground to observe their leadership and influence skills in an area where they don't have direct ownership of the process or the personnel.

An effective practice that is becoming more common is requiring that managerial candidates have formal improvement experience, meaning time spent as a Master Black Belt, Black Belt, or even Green Belt.

In the Black Belt role, a typical plan is that the candidate will spend an 18- to 24-month rotation in the improvement role to broaden her exposure to other business areas and develop this new and useful skill set. It is an opportunity to test the individual's leadership potential. At the end of the cycle, assuming good performance, the person is considered for leadership positions.

However, since you can't predict what will be happening in your organization when someone's rotation ends, we advise companies *not* to promise particular jobs or timelines. The best you can do is to make improvement experience a high-priority criterion for managerial candidates.

Also note that you can have confidence in making those promises only if you truly select top candidates for your core improvement positions. If the people taking those positions think they will become managerial candidates, and it turns out that the organization never had that intention, all you'll do is create employee dissatisfaction.

The more you populate your leadership tiers with people who have come to naturally think in terms of teamwork, data, and improvement, the deeper those values will take root in your organization. Over time, the culture is changed to become more customer-centric, data-driven, and process-focused by the influence of these new leaders.

A POSITIVE DYNAMIC

What organization would *not* want to do a better job of meeting customer expectations? Or *not* want to make better decisions based on data . . . or *not* want to encourage people who were dedicated to continuous improvement? How could these things *not* help improve business results? The values and behaviors that support Lean Six Sigma are also those that create a more innovative, adaptive, and competitive business.

This positive dynamic, where Lean Six Sigma values strengthen the business and vice versa, typically grows slowly. As your deployment evolves—from the early stages, where individuals begin trying something new, to later stages, where teams, departments, and eventually the organization as a whole get involved—you will gradually become more attuned to behaviors that support an improvement-oriented culture and those that impede progress.

Ultimately, you will reach a point where your organization's culture and the Lean Six Sigma culture are one and the same. And that's when you'll be positioned for high performance.

4

Measuring Progress and Success

With Lisa Custer, PhD

In God we trust. All others must bring data.
—W. Edwards Deming

A deployment leader at a Fortune 500 oil and gas company was frustrated with the progress of the company's new Lean Six Sigma deployment. While there were a number of success stories from great individual projects, the general pace of project completion wasn't meeting the organization's expectations. The deployment leader needed more information to get to the root cause of the issue.

The original project monitoring was ad hoc by department, and it was difficult to get a consistent, high-level view. The deployment leader consulted with his team members and implemented a dashboard that included information about project financials, phase status, and cycle times. From the dashboard, he saw that one department was struggling with long Measure phases, and he wondered whether this was because of a lack of data availability. Another department was having false starts as a result of poor project selection, leading to slow completion rates. The dashboard provided the data required to have a fact-based conversation in areas where improvement was needed. It also highlighted successes that could be celebrated more broadly.

One of the core tenets of Lean Six Sigma is that as far as possible, decisions should be grounded in data. That tenet holds true just as much for managing and evaluating the overall deployment as it does for making decisions concerning any individual project. Metrics serve a number of vital functions, including determining the value of projects relative to each other, describing the context for understanding the impact of a problem, and providing a scorecard for measuring success.

Knowing how results will be measured means knowing how performance will be evaluated. But outcome or results metrics are lagging indicators; they reflect the past. They do not allow the deployment leader to understand and manage what is happening today so that he can improve the results metrics tomorrow. To do that, the leader needs leading indicators—data that help him monitor progress and identify potential trouble areas. Leading indicators are used to make the countless decisions needed to manage a deployment: Can the organization handle the number of projects that are being launched? Should there be more or fewer projects? How is the training effort proceeding? What is the value of the projects represented by the portfolio? What is the participation in the program across functions or geographies?

This chapter discusses both kinds of metrics—those used to evaluate success and those used to manage performance—and talks about different ways in which companies use metrics to manage their Lean Six Sigma deployments.

MEASURING OUTPUTS

Organizations launch Lean Six Sigma initiatives because they are looking for particular outcomes or results. With rare exceptions, one of those outcomes is a return that indicates that the initiative is, at a minimum, paying for itself—and most initiatives are expected to generate returns many times greater than the investment. That means that no matter what the main purpose of a deployment may be, most companies want to have a dollar amount that will help them decide whether the effort is worth it. If nothing else, they need to be able to balance the benefits they see against the costs expended to generate the results. Those benefits can be measured in dollars, but less tangible factors (such as improved safety, morale, or customer satisfaction) often come into play as well.

The outcome metrics used to evaluate a Lean Six Sigma deployment can be divided into two categories:

1. *Business metrics.* Measure the value of the projects to the organization in terms of:
   - Revenue generation
   - Cost reduction
   - Asset reduction (e.g., inventory reduction)
2. *Process metrics.* Measure the performance of the process as directly experienced by the customer and the business. These typically fall into the following categories:
   - Quality (e.g. yield, on-time delivery, percent rework)
   - Speed (cycle time)
   - Cost or process efficiency (e.g., labor hours per invoice, cost per delivery, units produced per employee, units produced per hour)
   - Environmental, health, and safety
   - Regulatory compliance

These two kinds of metrics are related: good process performance (as measured by process metrics) drives good business performance (as measured by business metrics). A key issue for every deployment is which kind of metrics will be used to measure the benefits at the project level. The deployment leader should also think about how these gains will show up on a P&L statement and what non-P&L gains will be tracked. Defining these metrics for your organization is the first step.

Working Closely with Finance

Since every company involved with Lean Six Sigma needs to track costs and benefits, take the time to forge strong links between key deployment participants and the finance department up front, so that there is a common understanding of how both benefits and costs will be measured. Depending on the size of the deployment, it is helpful to identify one or more finance representatives who will work with the Lean Six Sigma team on an ongoing basis.

Early on, for example, have your deployment champion invite the representatives from the finance department to work with those involved in leading or tracking projects. The goal will be to make sure that everyone understands how project benefits and costs will be defined and measured. For example, the finance team can explain which lines in a P&L statement should be affected (positively or negatively) as a result of the various projects.

Once the framework has been established, it is typically the job of the sponsor and the Belt to suggest an approach for calculating the benefits of a specific project, and also to provide an initial estimate. The finance representative then either validates that this estimate is correct or adjusts it as needed.

The system your company sets up for measuring benefits should have at least the following three components:

1. Definition of benefit categories
2. Description of how to calculate benefits
3. Financial and other measurable objectives for each project

Definition of Benefit Categories

Most organizations today recognize that some benefits are easily measured, but that less tangible benefits might be equally important. So they will try to capture different types of benefits, defined by their potential to affect the income statement and balance sheet and the certainty with which you can establish the cause-and-effect relationship (Figure 4.1).

FIGURE 4.1 Benefit types

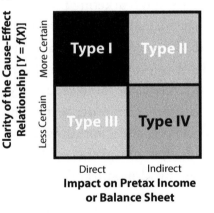

We define these categories as follows:

- *Type I.* Benefits that have a direct impact on the bottom line, and for which there is a clear cause-and-effect relationship between the project and the resulting gain that can be quantified and measured. Examples include permanent elimination or addition of revenue, cost, capital, or inventory, compared to a baseline.

- *Type II.* Benefits that do not immediately affect the P&L figures, but that are expected to have a positive effect in the long run. This includes more efficient or effective use of baseline resources, but no actual change in baseline pretax income or the balance sheet. Examples include reallocation of resources, cost and capital avoidance, and redeployment of a capital asset to an area with a demonstrated need.

- *Type III.* Benefits that generally create direct potential opportunities for future revenue growth, but where the cause-and-effect relationship is less certain. Examples include increased revenue due to faster time to market of new products and services, or increased revenue due to improved sales and marketing processes.

- *Type IV.* Benefits that help the organization strategically and over the long term, but that are typically difficult to quantify or to prove cause and effect. Examples could be increased safety, improved regulatory compliance, or customer satisfaction improvements. This category also includes benefits that do not show up on the P&L during the designated time period for tracking, which is usually within 12 months of the end of a project's Control phase.

Early in a deployment, the organization's leaders need to set goals for what percentage of projects should lie in each category. If cost reduction is the primary goal of your program, then most of your projects should fall into the Type I category. For example, a large hospitality company was interested in demonstrating a fast return on its investment in Lean Six Sigma. Realizing that it would be very difficult to have *all* Type I projects, it set its goal as 90 percent of projects to be Type I in the first year. The first-year results showed the value of the initiative by returning double the investment. In subsequent years, the ratio was changed to broaden the types of projects in the portfolio. While still keeping an emphasis on financial returns, the company added quite a few projects that were focused on customer satisfaction.

Note, however, that not all companies can have a large percentage of Type I projects. It is those companies whose costs are mainly direct (and found in the COGS line of an income statement) that usually have an easier time finding Type I savings. Companies whose costs are predominantly SG&A will have a more difficult time generating Type I savings unless they want to reduce headcount. An example is a financial services company that wanted to improve its customers' experience. The company ran a project that reduced the time to open new accounts by 75 percent.

While the customers appreciated the significant *time* savings, translating that into either a *cost* savings or a *revenue* enhancement for the company was difficult and certainly fell into an indirect category. Achieving working capital savings through better inventory and cash management is a financial opportunity at many companies. The point here is to set reasonable goals for your deployment and adapt those goals over time.

Description of How to Calculate Net Benefits

Once the factors are defined, you should describe the method that will be used to calculate the net benefit, meaning a figure that takes both costs and benefits into account. Different companies treat costs very differently (see sidebar), addressing issues such as whether one-time costs (for equipment, software, and the like) and deployment costs (such as for training) will be factored in.

What About Costs?

Companies take different approaches to addressing Lean Six Sigma costs.

As with most endeavors, payroll costs are often the largest expense associated with Lean Six Sigma projects. However, those are costs that the company pays whether or not the people are working on improvements. Further, since team members rarely work full-time on a single project, trying to track the percentage of time a team member spends on supporting a Lean Six Sigma project has proved extraordinarily difficult and is generally not worth the effort.

What some companies do is treat ongoing staffing costs (the Belt positions, for example) the same way they treat other internal payroll costs. Training costs are viewed as a one-time investment that will be compared against benefits a year or two down the road. Some companies also choose to track "special deployment costs" for items—software, equipment, and so on—that they might not otherwise have purchased, but others simply weave those costs into other operating budgets.

In short, your senior leadership (including the finance department) and the deployment leadership should discuss up front which costs, if any, will be specifically allocated to a deployment budget or treated in some other way.

Also, an important issue when calculating project benefits is defining the time horizon that you will use—that is, how long after project completion will benefits be tracked and credited to the project? Often, companies will do an immediate estimate of costs and benefits when the project concludes, followed by a validation measurement at least six months and perhaps a year or longer down the road. After the project is completed, a 12-month timeline for benefit calculation is typical.

Financial and Other Measurable Objectives for Each Project

For most companies, establishing financial and other measurable objectives for the initial projects is usually more art than science; the deployment champion or project sponsors will set goals based on what they would like to see happen. As the company completes more projects, however, it should get better at setting objectives because people will understand what other similar projects have been able to produce.

Calculating the Net Worth of the Portfolio

Balancing out the expected gains and expected costs from all of the projects allows you to establish an expectation concerning overall gains from a deployment effort.

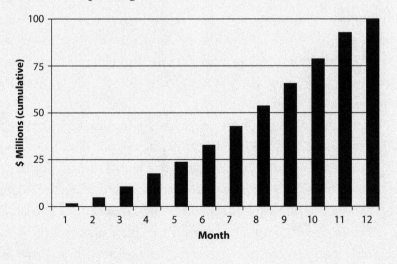

FIGURE 4.2 Expected gains

MEASURING INPUTS: THE METRICS OF DEPLOYMENT MANAGEMENT

Another core tenet of Lean Six Sigma is that you can't manage results if you look only at output metrics. To produce better results, you have to know what is going *into* the process. The relationship between outputs and inputs is often captured in the formula

$$Y = f(X)$$

This formula indicates that any output you see (the Y) is determined by (or "is a function of") the inputs, the Xs. More specifically, there will be a "critical few" Xs that will have the biggest impact on the results you can achieve. This simple formula holds true for any process or operation, no matter how large or how small.

The most common application of this concept in a Lean Six Sigma deployment is looking at the relationship between the desired results of an individual project, the Y, such as savings, and the process inputs, or Xs, that shape that output (process steps, information flow, supplies, and so on).

However, an equally important application of this concept is thinking about how to manage the deployment to generate better overall results. What are the inputs (Xs) to the deployment that will help shape the outcome? Typical data used to help manage a deployment, especially in the early stages, focus on activities started rather than results achieved.

Going into all the options for what Xs to measure is beyond the scope of this book. One way to think about your data needs as they relate to deployment management is to identify the questions you'll have to address. This often includes issues such as: Can the organization handle the number of projects being launched, or should there be more or fewer? How is the training effort proceeding? What is the value of the projects represented by the portfolio? What is the participation in the program across functions or geographies? What areas are having success? What areas are falling short? Are high-potential candidates being chosen for Belt positions?

Some of these questions are more easily answered than others, but data have a role to play in all of them. Every organization will probably have a different set of questions that are most critical to answer, and that will shape the decisions about what metrics to track. Here are some typical examples of deployment management metrics:

- Number of people trained per month, monthly and cumulative numbers (see Figure 4.3)
- Number of projects launched
  - Number of projects completed
  - Number of projects currently active
  - Often coded by type of project (kaizen, DMAIC, or design)

The upper chart in Figure 4.3 shows that the initial training focus was on leadership and Black Belts, followed by Green Belts, and then specialized training on different methodologies (including kaizen). This kind of chart helps to ensure that the launch plan is on track. You can see that the training figures vary by month, generally falling off nearer the end of the year, which was expected. Every deployment will probably see something similar—an initial push to get people trained, followed by results, possibly with a repeated pattern if cycles of training are conducted each year.

The lower chart in Figure 4.3 is one way to capture the cumulative human or people investment in training, which is one item that a deployment champion would want to report to senior leadership.

These kinds of charts are especially relevant when there are corporate or department goals involving training or implementation, or when the company has a staged rollout and wants to make sure that progress is tracking with the training plan. They can also be used as evidence of employee development.

FIGURE **4.3** Example of training data

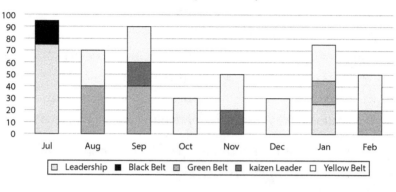

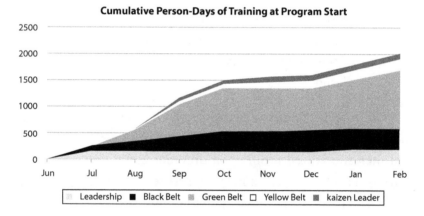

Signs of Cultural Change

Data on the scope of training are often used as a stand-in metric to indicate the potential for cultural change. The more people who have been trained, the more likely it is that Lean Six Sigma concepts and techniques will become embedded in everyday work and not just used for special occasions.

As much as possible, metrics on the status of a deployment should include the target or expected results versus the actual figures (an example is shown later in this chapter). Table 4.1 describes typical types of data tracked for a typical project and how those data are used.

TABLE **4.1** Project management data

Information	How Used
Name and title of project sponsor	• Provides contact information for questions about the project • Identifies early adopters
Location (geographic, department, and/or function)	• Identifies replication opportunities • Tracks the spread of Lean Six Sigma methodologies • Ensures that all departments and geographic areas are participating as expected
Name of the project leader and the date he was trained	• Provides contact information for questions about the project • Data on training helps document the experience of project leaders
Start and end dates of projects (cycle times) Optional but recommended: start and end dates of each DMAIC phase	• We recommend tracking overall project cycle times (see Figure 4.4). This allows the deployment leaders to evaluate whether teams are working as quickly as expected and react if project times start to lag • Many companies also track the start and end dates of each phase of DMAIC so that they can evaluate how quickly projects complete each step and also where there might be issues
Key words	• Allows people accessing the database to find specific projects or projects that fit certain criteria • Helps identify project replication opportunities • Typical key words describe the target of the project (such as "manufacturing project on the XYZ line" or "customer satisfaction project in New York")
Benefits expected versus those gained (especially Type I and Type II)	• Used to evaluate the gains from a project • Over time, helps to improve estimates • Used for calculating overall financial metrics

FIGURE 4.4 Project cycle times

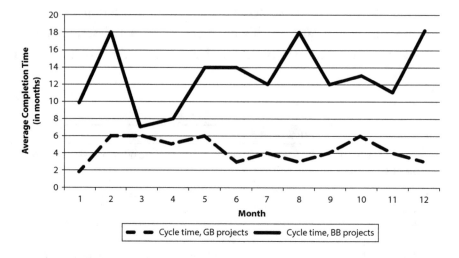

Figure 4.4 shows that Green Belt projects take about 4 months on average, while Black Belt projects are averaging closer to 13 months. Whether this is good or bad depends on the circumstances and the scope of the projects being assigned. In this case, the figures met the company's expectations. However, if the company wanted shorter projects, it could make adjustments in its system (scope, resource allocation, and so on) and use this kind of chart to see whether project cycle times improved.

SETTING UP THE DATA GATHERING SYSTEM

Deciding how to track the benefits and costs associated with projects is not always straightforward. Typically, companies will make a best effort at defining and developing their metrics up front, then build in checkpoints where they can refine and revise their definitions as needed so that they gradually get more precise.

Identifying what you need to measure if you are to capture costs and benefits is the starting point for developing a data-gathering system. Your system can be simple or complex, depending on the needs of the organization. Some companies use dedicated project-tracking systems (such as Instantis or PowerSteering), but many just establish a set of Excel spreadsheets that link to their financial records. We recommend beginning with a simple approach when the deployment is just getting started.

The overall system of metrics should be owned by the deployment champion. If you have multiple deployment champions, each should keep her own scorecard, but they should all use the same metrics, calculated in the same way, so that the numbers can be summed or compared as needed. Other people will need to be involved in entering data and preparing reports in whatever system your team selects.

Logistically, the project sponsor is usually responsible for preparing an initial estimate of what a project is worth, and making sure that this amount is entered into the database. These estimates should be done as the very first step—before any projects are launched—so that you will have a baseline on the results metrics that are going to be integrated into the P&L statements. In some companies, the needed data can be found in historical records—but you have to make sure that the figures were calculated using the same definitions that are being used for the deployment. If relevant historical data are not available, then train an appropriate person on how to gather and enter the data, and have that person apply the methods to establish baseline measurements on key metrics.

Once the project is active, the project leader or project sponsor will enter the project data into a database as they are generated. Identify a measurement frequency that makes sense for you. Typically, the sponsor or team leader will meet with the financial department contact to go through the numbers at four points:

1. The beginning of the project, to verify the original estimate of benefits.

2. The end of the Measure phase, when the baseline for all key metrics has been established.
3. In the Control phase, after the project has been completed (to verify actual costs and validate benefits).
4. An additional validation point is also recommended, either 6 or 12 months after project completion, to confirm that the gains were maintained.

The Balanced Scorecard

You've probably heard the term *balanced scorecard* in relation to managing a business. The method can be applied in managing a Lean Six Sigma deployment as well. The concept is to develop a short list of key metrics that will allow the top leadership to quickly understand the status of a deployment. Balanced scorecards typically include a handful of both success metrics (lagging indicators) and performance metrics (leading indicators).

CASE 1: THE 100-DAY PLAN

The CEO of a multinational corporation with nearly 30,000 employees worldwide took the stance that if he got Lean Six Sigma embedded in the culture and rewarded people for producing results, then significant benefits would accrue. Recognizing that measurable benefits would take time to show up on financial statements, his focus during the first 100 days was on deployment metrics. These metrics allowed him and the deployment champion to see how quickly and deeply

Lean Six Sigma training was penetrating into different departments and localities. They wanted to know, for example:

- How many people had been trained and participated in projects
- Where the training participants were coming from (manufacturing versus operations, geographical dispersion, and so on)
- Key aspects of each project's charter (proposed, approved, functional area, value)

For this company, these metrics were first used to evaluate the level of participation in different geographic regions around the globe (North America versus Europe versus Asia Pacific, for example). The company determined that participation was uneven, and the CEO used those data to set participation goals for the following year—expectations that he made clear to the presidents in each region!

CEO Support

The CEO of this company often starts off employee meetings by asking, "How many of you have served on a Lean Six Sigma project team?" This simple step reinforces the idea that participation in Lean Six Sigma and the skills gained by doing so are considered important to this company. His constant emphasis on the value of Lean Six Sigma experience is helping to shift the culture quickly.

As the deployment matured, this company also began looking at the number of new projects that were spun off from completed projects. It discovered that nearly every project opens doors to further improvement opportunities, and that people who have been successful with one project are often inspired to tackle additional ideas. Their mentality switches from, "Oh, no, we have another problem," to, "I see some more problems that I could solve." In short, the number of spin-off projects was a good indicator of the level of enthusiasm among employees.

CASE 2: MANAGEMENT AND RESULTS

A large Asian multinational company set up a system to track a number of deployment metrics for the first year after launch, coupled with results measurements that would be ongoing. The deployment plan included an up-front training phase that would last about six months, during which pilot projects were launched. The company knew that measurable benefits would probably not appear until some months after the first projects were completed.

The pilot projects were launched in July and August in conjunction with the training. You can see this reflected in Figure 4.5, with most projects being in the Define and Measure phases in those first months. Gradually, more and more projects move into the later phases (Analyze, Improve, and Control). The first project was completed the following January.

Imagine that you were the deployment champion, watching the chart in Figure 4.5 build month by month. If you saw that the Measure or the Analyze segment remained large for several months in a row, that would indicate that projects were stalling out, and you could investigate to find out why.

FIGURE **4.5** Project tracking by phase

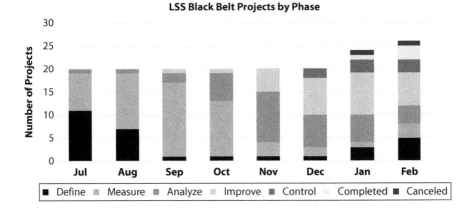

Another way to track projects is shown in Figure 4.6, which depicts the expected savings by project type for the first six months of the calendar year. Actual savings are plotted against these expectations to make sure that the different types of projects are delivering the expected results that are built into P&L forecasts.

FIGURE **4.6** Estimated savings by project type

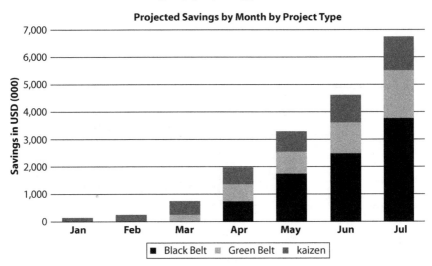

Value of the Project Portfolio

As companies get more experienced, they usually get to a point where they can estimate the value of each project with some accuracy. That, in turn, allows the deployment champion to provide senior leaders with an estimate of the overall value of the project portfolio.

Another way this company tracked progress is shown in Figure 4.7, which depicts the expected versus the actual number of active projects in each month. As you can see, the actual number of projects launched started to fall further and further behind the projections as time went on. After seeing this pattern continue, the deployment champion launched a mini-DMAIC project to investigate why. With the metrics data available, the project team was able to look at issues such as whether the problem was the same across

FIGURE 4.7 Actual versus projected number of projects

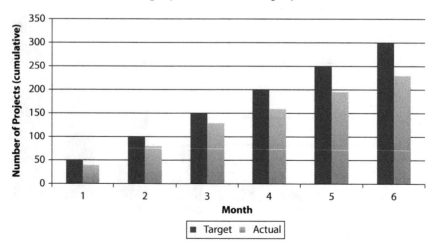

all divisions and geographies or affected only a few, and whether the issue was the same for all project types (kaizen, Green Belt, or Black Belt). Without this kind of data, the deployment champion might not have realized that there was a problem until much later in the deployment.

No Measurement, No Management

There's an old saying that if you can't measure something, you can't manage it. Practitioners of Lean Six Sigma know that this statement is at least partly true. Data in the form of metrics provides vital information that is needed to create a successful deployment. If your organization does not track success metrics, you won't be able to evaluate the value of the contribution that Lean Six Sigma is making to your business goals. If you don't track deployment metrics, you won't know how to best manage your resources or be able to correct problems before they show up on the bottom line.

There are many different metrics that can be used to track hard measures of success (such as the dollar value of the project portfolio) and what you might think of as the cultural side of success (such as how widely the tools and methods are being used). Both types of metrics are needed to shape a productive deployment. We recommend beginning with a simple approach when the deployment is just getting started and enhancing it as the deployment matures.

Also, don't expect to be perfect up front. Typically, companies will initially make a good-faith effort to define metrics that make sense, knowing that they will need to evaluate those metrics throughout the deployment. Over time, the definitions of what the metrics represent and how to gather the appropriate data can be made more precise.

As good as your metric system becomes, however, remember the advice of W. Edwards Deming, who recognized decades ago that managing by numbers alone is not sound leadership. Yes, you need the numbers, but you also need to consider intangibles such as enthusiasm and morale among both employees and customers when you are managing a deployment and evaluating its impact. So make sure you get good data, but temper the interpretation of those data with judgment and experience.

5

The Art and Science of Project Selection and Pipeline Management

"We haven't been very successful at convincing managers to support our Lean Six Sigma deployment." "We're not seeing the kind of payback on our investment that everyone had hoped." "We haven't moved the dial on our key metrics." "We're not getting good candidates in our Black Belt training." "Our Black Belts keep getting pulled out before their projects are done." "We have to scramble to find projects for all of our Black Belt trainees." "We have so many good ideas that our Black Belts are overloaded with projects."

You've probably heard some of these kinds of complaints about Lean Six Sigma initiatives before; you may even have voiced them yourself. While each complaint could have multiple causes, *all* of them are also symptoms of problems with project selection and management.

Companies that don't create a pipeline of high-priority projects have no option but to accept any reasonable-sounding idea that comes along. That sets off a vicious cycle: If projects aren't linked directly to business priorities, they won't produce results that are meaningful to managers or executives, so they won't move key metrics. No one will want to invest in something that isn't creating value, so the company will have a hard time getting buy-in. Managers won't be willing to assign top performers to Lean Six Sigma positions, and won't see project work as a priority compared to other deadlines. They won't put in the time needed to identify meaningful projects— and the downward spiral continues.

If companies don't *manage* their project pipeline correctly, they are likely to overload their Black Belts with too many projects and give them too few resources. When there's no way the teams can keep all their assigned projects moving forward, the projects will take too long or the results will be compromised in some way. Managers then get frustrated by the lack of timely or meaningful results, leading to the downward spiral just described.

To get the best results from your Lean Six Sigma initiative, you need to master the skills of creating *and* managing a project pipeline. As we'll talk about in this chapter, the first requirement is making sure that you can clearly tie the projects in the pipeline to business priorities. The second requirement is managing the pipeline so that projects get done as quickly as possible without sacrificing the quality of results.

Meeting both requirements delivers a number of benefits, such as getting timely results on significant projects that matter to the organization and all the good things that cascade out from that (Figure 5.1).

Creating and managing a pipeline of high-quality projects requires a mix of science and art. In this chapter, we'll first cover the three phases of project identification and prioritization: ideation, prioritization/selection, and chartering (as shown in Figure 5.2). Afterward, we'll discuss how to manage the pipeline of project ideas that you've just created in order to increase the chances of having the shortest possible project cycle times with the most meaningful project results.

FIGURE 5.1 Benefits of effective project selection

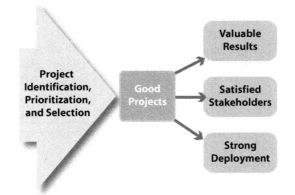

FIGURE 5.2 Project identification and selection process overview

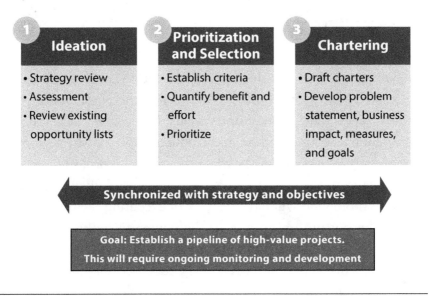

PHASE 1: IDEATION

Coming up with project ideas is typically done through either a top-down or a bottom-up approach. Both have strengths and weaknesses, as summarized in Table 5.1. In a top-down approach, you start by looking at the business as a whole, often including an assessment

TABLE 5.1 Top-Down vs. Bottom-Up project identification

	Top-Down	Bottom-Up
Approach	Assessment or analysis-based, tied to overall business strategy	Projects identified from within the business, at all levels. Typically come from existing data—customer complaints, quality issues, or employee suggestions
Benefits	Data-driven identification, with clear link to strategic drivers	Convenience, relevance to an individual's daily work
Challenges	Requires up-front analysis and planning. May require a higher level of resources to run the project	Must determine how the projects tie back to the overall business strategy. Fewer cross-functional or transformational projects

of how the company is performing relative to its strategic goals. Looking at the business this way allows you to think about what is most important for the business overall, and therefore identify high-value projects that are important to business leaders. This approach does require devoting effort and resources up front to performing a thorough assessment. Also, while the potential projects may have relevance to top leaders, they may not be easily linked to the daily work of those who will have the task of executing them.

In the bottom-up approach, the company looks through the existing data and solicits ideas from people in different areas of the business. This approach is relatively easy because most business units either already have lists of existing problems or opportunities or can create them quickly just by brainstorming with employees. The upside of this approach is that you know you're identifying areas that are of direct concern to employees. The downside is that these ideas often don't have a clear link to the business's priorities or strategy. The other limitation of the bottom-up approach is that it's difficult to identify cross-functional or transformational projects that could have a major impact across large portions of the business.

Since both approaches have their limitations, the most effective strategy blends the two. Start with a top-down assessment of your business so that you can link Lean Six Sigma projects to strategic priorities, then link projects to frontline concerns by adding some bottom-up perspectives from people at different levels of the organization. We'll go into more detail on both of these elements next.

Assessments

In the context of Lean Six Sigma, the goal of an assessment is to identify problems or opportunities that can be addressed through improvement projects. Figure 5.3 shows an overview of the assessment process, which includes up-front planning, data collection through interviews, analysis of the value stream map, and then synthesis of all the information to generate potential project ideas.

Exploring this process in depth would require a book of its own. For our purposes here, we want to focus on something that many companies overlook: the diversity of skills and expertise that contributes to a successful assessment. Collectively, the team working on your assessment needs to have expertise in these four areas:

1. Connecting with management and leadership
2. Interviewing
   - Determining how many people should be interviewed
   - Selecting candidates that represent a good cross section of perspectives and needs
   - Developing a set of questions that will elicit the right kinds of information, and customizing them for the audience (executives, directors, managers, or frontline staff)

FIGURE 5.3 Assessment process overview

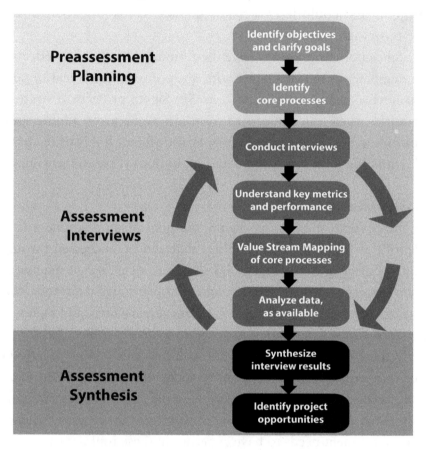

3. Working with processes
   - Identifying core processes
   - Developing and analyzing value stream maps
   - Identifying appropriate process metrics
4. Data analysis and synthesis
   - Analyzing relevant business, process, and customer data
   - Synthesizing all data to identify project opportunities
   - Working with leaders to identify project opportunities based on the overall synthesis of results

If you have people internally who have most or all of these skills, put them in charge of overseeing and planning the assessment. However, don't hesitate to look outside your area (different departments or outside firms) to fill in any skill gaps. An assessment team with an outside perspective typically generates more potential project ideas, as it can be challenging for a business area to see where its own processes are in need of improvement.

From Ideas to Projects

The interviews and process analysis are likely to reveal a large number of improvement opportunities. From there, you have to synthesize what you learn in order to identify ideas that could be addressed through projects, and further reduce the list to those projects that can best be addressed with the Lean Six Sigma methodology (Figure 5.4).

FIGURE 5.4 From ideas to projects

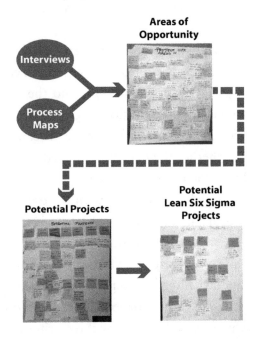

To give you an idea of how science and art come together to generate project ideas, here is an example from a recent analysis that we conducted:

- From the interviews, we learned that a process owner felt that his process was doing "great" because the goal was to complete orders within 60 days, and on average they were at 24 days. However, another manager working in the same area told us that in an upcoming reorganization, the department was adding 10 people because customers were complaining that the process took too long. This second person wondered whether 10 was the right number of additional resources.
- Data analysis showed that there was a lot of variation in the process. While the average completion time was 24 days, there was a long tail on the distribution (so a number of customers did indeed have reason to complain!). The data also showed that the "touch time" was only about 2 percent of the overall process cycle time; the rest was lost in wait time.

There were obvious contradictions between the owner's impression that the process was doing "great," the need to add people because "customers were complaining," and the data on variation. This led to a project focused on deciding whether "under 60 days" was the right target, understanding why the process varied so greatly, and determining whether the department needed to add staff, and if so, whether 10 was the right number.

Comparing people's impressions with the data will often expose contradictions, as in this case, or at least help identify priority areas where further investigation is needed.

Once you have synthesized all your information to come up with project ideas, the last filter is determining whether they should be addressed with Lean Six Sigma or some other methodology. Potential Lean Six Sigma projects need to meet three criteria:

1. The starting point should be identifying a problem that does not have a known solution. If the solution is known or is very simple, there's no need to do the extensive problem and solution analysis that's embedded in the Lean Six Sigma methodology; a simple "just do it" type of project will probably suffice.

2. There has to be a reasonable expectation of delivering significant value to the organization in some way. "Value" might mean generating dollars in savings or cost avoidance, but it could also mean moving a strategic metric in a positive direction or improving a critical business process. Figure 5.5, for example, shows four potential projects identified by a financial services company that wanted to improve a key business metric, Customer Net Promoter Score.

3. You have to be able to tie the problem to a particular process, and you also want to identify the process owner. That person should be the project sponsor. Lean Six

FIGURE 5.5 Project ideas linked to a strategic need

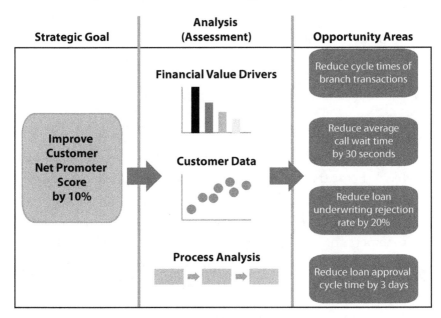

Sigma projects that are not "owned" by someone in line management run the risk of floundering because of a lack of support or because of not truly being a business priority.

After identifying potential projects, try to estimate their scope to make sure they can be completed within the targeted time frame (which is often four to six months for a full-blown DMAIC project, although it could be longer). If the potential projects can be done much more quickly than in four to six months, and you don't feel they would benefit from a full DMAIC analysis, they may be better treated as "quick hit" projects. If you think they'll take a lot longer, look for ways to scale them down. Long project times lead to all sorts of problems, not the least of which is a failure to produce results!

By the end of this phase, you should have a list of potential projects that:

- Are important to business leaders because they are tied to a business need.
- Are linked to a process that needs improvement.
- Have a potential project sponsor identified (ideally, the process owner).
- Can be completed within the target specific time frame.

An Additional Criterion for First Projects

If you are looking for projects to assign to novice Green or Black Belts, try to choose something that has the possibility of using a wide selection of Lean Six Sigma tools. Exposing Belts to a range of tools and methods when they have access to expert coaches (trainers for their courses or Master Black Belts) can speed up the learning curve and better prepare them to handle future projects on their own.

PHASE 2: PRIORITIZATION AND SELECTION

The goal of Phase 2 is to convert the list of potential opportunities into a hopper of prioritized ideas that you can draw from as needed. The process, shown schematically in Figure 5.6, is usually based on a benefit/effort evaluation.

FIGURE 5.6 Prioritization process

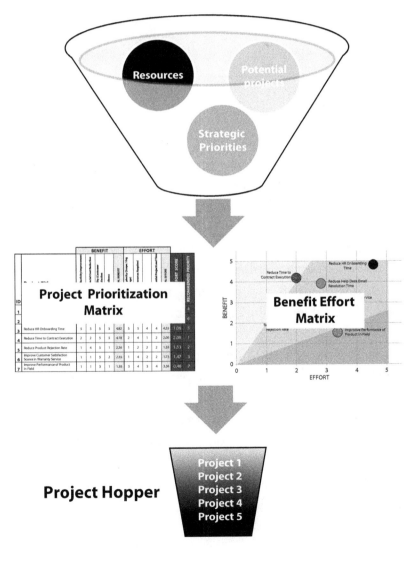

The initial step in this phase is to establish the benefit and effort criteria by which your leadership team will judge each project. Common types of criteria are shown in Table 5.2; you will want to develop customized criteria and definitions to fit your situation. (Benefit calculations were discussed further in Chapter 4.)

TABLE 5.2 Common types of criteria

Benefit Criteria	Effort Criteria
• Cost savings	• Time to complete
• Revenue growth	• Number of resources required
• Safety improvement	• Capital investment
• Environmental impact	• Risk

You will also want to weight the criteria to align them with your business strategies. For example, if "reducing cycle times" is the most important metric, you would weight that criterion more heavily than something like "reducing defects" or even "cost savings." Typically, weighting is done by the leadership team and tied to organizational strategy.

To eliminate the need for making judgment calls on the scoring, it works best to define three levels for each criterion, usually labeled low, medium, and high and given the numbers 1, 3, and 5, respectively. Table 5.3 shows an example that one company created for its benefit scoring. As you can see, the table shows low, medium, and high levels for four different types of benefits (savings, revenue, safety, and environment). This company prepared a similar table for the effort criteria that it identified.

Once you have the criteria, the leadership team can work to complete a project prioritization matrix, which is structured to compare the total effort and benefit of different ideas. The version we use leads to numerical results that can easily be ranked. A schematic of the matrix is shown in Figure 5.7.

TABLE 5.3 Example definitions of benefit criteria

	Score	Cost Savings ($000)	Revenue Growth ($000)	Safety Improvement	Environmental Impact
Low	1	≤$500	≤$2,000	Affects one root cause of "lost time due to injury"	Slight improvement
Medium	3	$500 ≤ $1,000	$2,000 ≤ $5,000	Affects more than one root cause of "lost time due to injury"	Moderate improvement
High	5	>$1,000	>$5,000	Affects a safety issue that poses a risk of death	Significant improvement

FIGURE 5.7 Project prioritization matrix

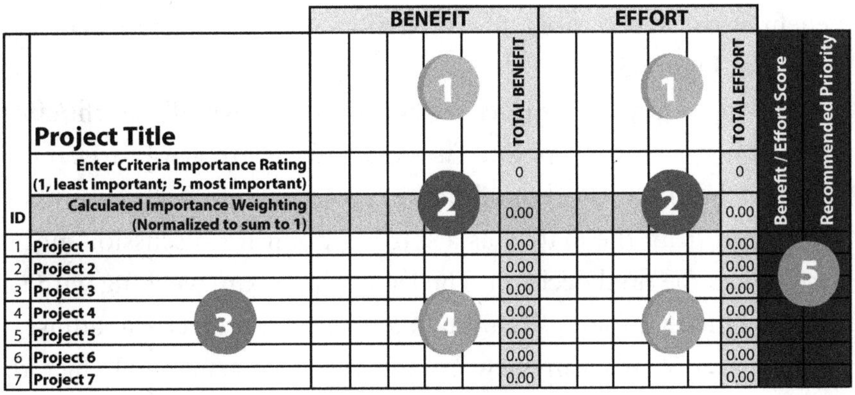

In the version of a prioritization matrix shown in Figure 5.7, you'll see all of the benefit and effort criteria (area 1) and the weightings that indicate relative importance (area 2). To complete the matrix, you list projects down the left (area 3), and then score them against each criterion (area 4). The scores are adjusted by the weight, then added together to come up with an overall

FIGURE 5.8 Completed prioritization matrix

ID	Project Title	Productivity Improvement	Financial Cost Reduction	Quality (Customer Satisfaction)	Timeliness	TOTAL BENEFIT	Complexity (Scope / Org Change)	# Resources Required	Cost	Potential ProjectLead Time	TOTAL EFFORT	BENEFIT/EFFORT SCORE	RECOMMENDED PRIORITY
		BENEFIT					**EFFORT**						
	Enter Criteria Importance Rating (1, least important; 5, most important)	2	1	3	5	11	5	1	2	3	11		
	Calculated Importance Weighting (Normalized to sum to 1)	0.18	0.09	0.27	0.45	1.00	0.45	0.09	0.18	0.27	1.00		
1	Reduce Help Desk E-mail Resolution Time	3	2	5	4	3.91	3	2	1	4	2.82	1.39	4
2	Improve Self-Service Capability and Utilization	5	4	3	2	3.00	4	2	2	3	3.18	0.94	6
3	Reduce HR Onboarding Time	5	3	5	5	4.82	5	5	4	4	4.55	1.06	5
4	Reduce Time to Contract Execution	2	2	5	5	4.18	2	4	1	2	2.00	2.09	1
5	Reduce Product Rejection Rate	1	4	5	1	2.36	1	2	2	2	1.55	1.53	2
6	Improve Customer Satisfaction Scores in Warranty Service	1	1	5	2	2.55	1	4	2	2	1.73	1.47	3
7	Improve Performance of Product in Field	1	1	3	1	1.55	3	4	3	4	3.36	0.46	7

benefit/effort score (area 5). A portion of a completed matrix is shown in Figure 5.8.

Having a list of projects ranked by their overall benefit/effort score is just a starting point. The calculations are a way to capture objective information about different projects, but the intent is to use the output from the matrix as a starting point for discussion, not to accept it as the final decision. The leadership team, working with the deployment champion, should talk about each project and adjust its ranking according to any new insights that they generate. In fact, the conversation among leaders about priorities is as important as the matrix. The real goal is to have all your leaders agree on the projects and their priorities. This ensures greater support going forward, and helps prevent internal disagreements about whose projects should go first or be given more resources. The result of these conversations is the final priority listing of potential projects.

Though not strictly necessary, it often helps to go one step further by plotting the benefit/effort scores of all potential projects on a

FIGURE 5.9 Benefit/effort chart

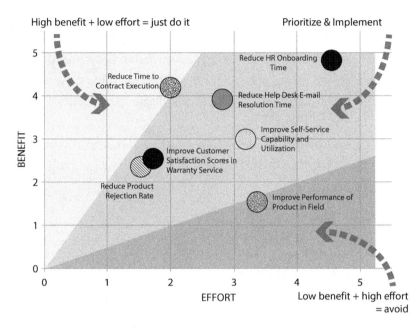

benefit/effort chart (Figure 5.9). Doing so provides a nice visual aid that facilitates the discussion. A benefit/effort chart helps you visually divide potential projects into three categories:

1. *Projects that are not good candidates because they provide little benefit for a lot of effort (lower right corner).* Don't discard these ideas entirely, but don't pursue them as long as you have project ideas with a better benefit/effort ratio. Many companies will revisit ideas in this category down the road and discover that perhaps their priority has increased, or perhaps the idea can be rescoped or reshaped in some way to produce more benefit (or at least the same benefit) for less effort.

2. *"Just do it" projects (upper left corner).* These projects are easy to do with relatively little effort. They may not require the full Lean Six Sigma treatment, but you should get them done because they provide good payback on little effort.

These projects may also be candidates for a more focused approach, known as a kaizen event.

3. *Best potential Lean Six Sigma projects (middle section).* These projects provide significant benefit compared to the effort needed to get the results. They should be considered the highest priority for Lean Six Sigma projects.

By the end of this phase, you should understand the priority of each potential project. You know which projects to launch first and which to save for later.

PHASE 3: PRELIMINARY CHARTERING

The final step before filling your project hopper is to capture some key information about the projects by starting to draft their charters. Typically, a completed charter will have six elements:

- Problem statement
- Measures and goals
- Scope
- Business impact
- Timeline
- Resources

All of these elements are subject to change once a project is officially launched and a team assigned, but you can kick-start the launch by having the project sponsor complete the first three elements at the end of the project identification work. This will help capture key information—such as *why* a project is a priority—while the reasoning is still fresh in the sponsor's mind. The idea is that when a project is activated, you will already have some basic information documented so that the team leader and the team assigned to the project can hit the ground running.

PROJECT LAUNCH AND PIPELINE MANAGEMENT

Even companies that are great at identifying and prioritizing project ideas often don't know how to regulate the launch of their projects so that they balance the need for results with the availability of resources. They often uncover many improvement opportunities through the project selection work and, in their eagerness to get them all done, assign each Black Belt to work on five, ten, or even more projects at once. There's no way anyone can work productively on that many projects at a time, and something has to give—cycle times, results, or quality. A good rule of thumb is to have a full-time Black Belt focus on only one project during his training, and then two or three projects at a time thereafter, depending on the scope of the projects and the Black Belt's other responsibilities.

The most effective way to manage a project pipeline is to treat it just like a manufacturing production line. Lean principles show how to optimize the productivity of any repetitive process through *Little's law*, which teaches us that the lead time of any process is determined by two factors: (1) how much work is currently in the process ("work in process" or WIP) and (2) how many items are completed over a given time period (the *average completion rate*). If you know these numbers, you can calculate the average lead time for any process using the very simple Little's law equation,

$$\text{Lead Time of Any Process} = \frac{\text{Number of "Things" in Process}}{\text{Average Completion Rate}}$$

What Little's law makes obvious—and what companies seldom think about—is that the amount of time it takes to complete any *single* project is affected by the *total number* of projects that are active at any given time. Let's say, for example, that your company has 30 active projects, and that on average you've been completing 10 projects every year. Little's law shows that the lead time of the process as a whole—the amount of time you should expect any individual project to take—is three years (= 30/10). Not great, right?

What could you do to speed up the lead time? Once again, Little's law provides the answer: you would have to either reduce the number of active projects (things in process) or speed up the completion rate. While it's possible to do the latter (for example, by assigning more resources to each project), the easiest solution by far is to simply reduce the number of active projects to a level that the workforce has the capacity to support. If you drop down to 10 active projects, the lead time drops from three years to one year (= 10/10).

The first rule about project pipeline management is to apply Little's law to control the number of active projects at any given time. Limiting the number of active projects allows you to close projects faster. In other words, don't overload your Black Belts. Trying to do too many projects all at once will slow down *all* projects.

Pulling Projects into the Pipeline

There's another concept from manufacturing that is useful for project pipeline management, that of a *pull system*. The principle behind a pull system is also very simple: work is released into a process *only* when some other work is completed. In terms of a project pipeline, that would mean that a project from the hopper of vetted ideas is launched only when another project is completed.

The way this works in project management is that you will determine the maximum number of projects you should have in development at any given time based on the Little's law calculation and the skills constraints of your workforce. Launch no more than that number of projects, starting with those that ranked highest in the final lists developed after the discussion of the prioritization matrix results. Only when one of those projects is completed should you reach into the hopper of unused ideas and pull out the next idea for launch.

For example, a large industrial equipment manufacturer studied the types of product development projects that it usually conducted and the skills required for those projects. The company determined that it could handle 3 large-scale product development projects and 20 smaller product upgrade projects simultaneously. The company then did a prioritization exercise on all active and proposed projects. It selected the top three development projects and put a hold on all other projects in the organization. Dedicated teams were assigned to each development project. Smaller projects were used to fill the capacity of team members who weren't being fully utilized. By focusing its development efforts in this way, the company's product development lead time went from 2.5 years to 9 months.

CONCLUSION

No aspect of Lean Six Sigma has a bigger impact on whether you see a good return on your investment than how you select ideas and manage your project pipeline. If you have a good process for identifying, selecting, and prioritizing the projects, you will get valuable results, have satisfied stakeholders, and ultimately produce a strong deployment. Managing the number of projects going on at any given time will keep project lead times low—meaning that you'll see faster results. And faster results not only help the bottom line, but build enthusiasm for improvement work among the participants and the management.

6

"How Are We Doing?"

Using a Maturity Model Assessment to Evaluate Where You Are and Where You Should Go Next

Every stage of a Lean Six Sigma initiative is beset by questions: Have we taken the right steps? Do we have the right pieces in place? Is anything missing? Where are we doing well? What are our challenges? What's most important for us to work on next?

All deployments involve these questions, so the smart thing to do is to anticipate them and take a proactive approach to finding some answers. One of the best ways to answer these questions is to periodically do an assessment, which can range from quick and easy to a more structured analysis.

At the quick and easy end of the spectrum is conducting a brief, open-ended survey where you ask the deployment participants questions about what's going well and what needs improvement. This approach is particularly useful for companies that have not assessed their deployment before. It helps them quickly understand where their biggest issues are from the perspective of the deployment participants.

The advantages of an open-ended survey are that it's quick and simple, and that you get a frontline perspective. But it has a number of limitations:

- There is nothing to compare yourself against except your past attempts. This makes it difficult to know whether the progress you've made is good or bad relative to other deployments.
- There are no objective ways to prioritize opportunities. You can compare the ideas you gather against business needs, but it's hard to compare them against one another and determine which might be more important.
- You know what ideas occurred to people, but you don't know what ideas *didn't* occur to them, so the results are biased by what captures people's attention. You can't be sure that you're not missing some important aspect of your deployment strategy.

Because of these limitations, we've worked with a number of companies to develop a tool that they can use to get more complete and objective information about where their deployment is doing well and what may need attention. The tool we developed falls into the category of *maturity models*, which are matrices that describe typical achievements possible at various stages of development along multiple dimensions of implementation.

When we first began this work, the best-known maturity model was CMMI, Capability and Maturity Model Integration, created by the Software Engineering Institute at Carnegie Mellon University. While its application has expanded, CMMI's initial goal was to improve software development. It allowed companies to evaluate their own status against a chart that provided a road map for improvement and to compare themselves against best practices from other industries. Our goal was to create a similarly useful maturity model for Lean Six Sigma.

In this chapter, we'll review key aspects of our Lean Six Sigma maturity model—its structure, its implementation, and evaluation of its results. Our goal is to show you how to answer the question, "How are we doing?" in a way that lets you continually improve your deployment.

MATURITY MODEL STRUCTURE

The purpose of a maturity model is to allow companies to evaluate how far they have progressed in a Lean Six Sigma deployment and chart a path forward. To fulfill that function, the model needs to spell out different components of a successful deployment, and also provide a way to gauge the stage of development. A maturity model is therefore a table or matrix listing the components of success on one dimension and the stages of achievement on the other. The framework of our model is shown in Figure 6.1.

As you can see, we've focused on five deployment components: strategy, projects, resources, training, and culture. These five make up the most important elements of a deployment, and you need to get them right if you are to have a successful initiative. Based on the precedents set by other maturity models, we also decided to use five levels of achievement or maturity, from the earliest stages of a grassroots effort with ad hoc projects to a world-class deployment.

Looking at the framework, it's clear that there are already 25 possible combinations (5 components with 5 levels for each). What we found, however, was that stopping at that level of definition was not adequate for a useful assessment. Knowing that you're a Level 3

FIGURE **6.1** Framework of our maturity model

Level Component	1 Introductory	2 Initial Results	3 Demon- strating Success	4 Successful Mature Deployment	5 Setting the Standard
Strategy					
Projects					
Resources					
Training					
Culture					

in strategy but only a Level 2 in resources, for example, doesn't help you decide what to do next. So we needed to take the maturity model down to the next level of detail, far enough that deployment teams could gain specific insights concerning where they stand now and what actionable opportunities they have available. However, we also knew that a maturity model couldn't be too complicated or people wouldn't use it.

In balancing the need for sufficient granularity with the need to keep the model relatively simple, we ended up defining 31 deployment elements divided among the five main components. We're not going to attempt to go through the entire matrix in this chapter; you can find it in Appendix A and on the Firefly Consulting website (www.firefly-consulting.com/publications) if you want to review the details.

For the purposes of this chapter, we'll talk a little more about each main component and the elements that were important enough to make it into the matrix, and indicate the thinking that goes into defining the levels. After that review, we'll talk about how to use the matrix as an assessment tool.

Growth Versus Stake in the Ground

As you read the following descriptions, keep in mind that for some elements, you will want to identify a growth model, such as starting with a "breakeven" goal for ROI and improving to a 10X return over several years. That is, you'll do best to think about working through the levels of maturity over time.

For other elements, you may simply want to put a stake in the ground at the level that best fits your business needs. For example, you may be able to select a top talent to serve as the deployment champion and give her a direct line of reporting to the CEO. That approach is considered best in class (Level 5). Or you might establish deployment wide metrics (Level 3) from the beginning, and understand that putting more effort into that dimension is not a priority at this point in the deployment.

Component 1: Strategy

As we discussed in Chapter 1, if you don't have the *why* right, you can end up making wrong decisions on all the other dimensions. That's why defining your strategy is always the most important aspect of a deployment. The strategy should describe why you are going to invest in Lean Six Sigma and what you want to accomplish, which in turn provides the impetus and direction necessary to generate business results that will justify continued investment of time and energy.

That means, for example, that if a manufacturing company's strategy is to make a significant increase in reliability, then its Lean Six Sigma projects should be focused on tackling the most meaningful reliability challenges. If a financial services company's major goal is to improve customer retention, then its Lean Six Sigma program should be making a significant contribution to customer satisfaction.

Beyond that overall direction, however, there are many other ways in which a deployment's contribution to strategy and goals can be evaluated. We talked about the basics of evaluating results in Chapter 4. In general, what you should see as a deployment matures is an increasing connection between what is important to the business and what is important to the program. If you have done a good job of defining a strategy for using Lean Six Sigma in your organization, each component of the deployment should evolve in alignment with those priorities as your initiative matures. For example:

- *Deployment alignment with business strategy.* In some grassroots deployments, strategic alignment is not considered. However, over time, companies with successful, mature deployments consider Lean Six Sigma to be a key methodology for the execution of the corporate strategy.
- *Breadth of deployment.* Many deployments start in a single geography or function, which is often an effective approach because it makes the deployment more manageable. But if the methods are successful there, one goal should be to spread them to other areas of the organization.
- *Leadership.* The bigger the impact you expect from your deployment, the higher up in the organization the leaders should be (both the deployment leader and the executive sponsors). And vice versa: the bigger the impact you can create, the more likely it is that influential leaders will become involved.
- *Total return on investment (ROI).* If financial returns are a critical factor for your organization, you should track the return on individual projects and on the overall deployment. In for-profit, publicly held businesses, significant benefits

must come fairly quickly, or else the leadership will lose interest. That means that the deployment should break even at first, then gradually increase to perhaps 5, 10, or even 20 times ROI as staff members get more experienced and your project selection process gets more refined. In some organizations, monetary gains, while still important, may not be the highest priority. For example, a space-flight operations company that we worked with had a strategy to make significant improvements in safety.

● *Metrics.* As we discussed in Chapter 4, the most important metrics while you are getting started with a deployment have to do with the inputs (number of people trained and number of projects launched, for example). As the deployment matures, the focus will shift more toward the outcome or results metrics that have been linked to the business priorities.

● *Finance participation.* The more important the Lean Six Sigma deployment is seen to be in the organization and the more substantial the deployment is in size, the more involved the finance department will be. This is a good thing. We want reported benefits to match actuals.

● *Linkage to performance planning.* Another indicator of how seriously a deployment is taken is the role that participation in Lean Six Sigma plays in performance evaluation and planning.

Component 2: Projects

As we discussed in Chapter 5, project selection can have a huge positive or negative effect on the success of a Lean Six Sigma deployment. The best deployments have a pipeline of valuable projects that are tied to the strategy of the business. If the project ideas are not good, there isn't any amount of wonderful execution that is going to make up for that problem. Weak results lead to a weakening of support, which sets off the vicious cycle described in Chapter 1.

As with the Strategy component, there are many factors that go into developing, maintaining, and managing a pipeline of high-quality projects. The first type of factor we look at is *measurable results*. There are many types of measurable results, as discussed in Chapter 4. For the purpose of evaluating a deployment, however, you will probably focus on three categories:

1. Overall measurable results of the program.
2. Financial results per Black Belt and per Green Belt project.
3. Cycle times per Black Belt and per Green Belt project. (Cycle-time tracking is frequently overlooked as a project success metric, but there is a big difference in practice between a $100,000 gain made in three months versus one made in two years.)

Predictably, the levels of development in each of these categories involve seeing greater returns from comparable investment as the organization gets more experienced with using Lean Six Sigma methods.

Another important aspect to examine is how projects are selected, executed, and managed to achieve maximum benefit. Some of these characteristics can be linked to the management metrics discussed in Chapter 4 (such as the training data), but you would also want to look at elements such as:

- *Tool rigor.* Is your organization using the right tools in the right places? How do you know? Are you tackling or shying away from projects that require advanced analysis techniques?
- *Control and sustainment.* In novice deployments, people are apt to view the end of the project as the end of their work. Experienced project staff members know that the end of a

project is just a signal for a new phase to commence—the hard work of making sure that the gains are sustained.

- *Replication.* One of the factors that allows experienced companies to get much more out of their Lean Six Sigma investments than novice companies is their ability to leverage every aspect of what they do. They take the lessons learned in one project and apply them to other projects in similar areas or using similar methods. They take an improvement in Location A and use it to improve Locations B, C, and D. With that kind of replication, they can get more out of every dollar they invest in Lean Six Sigma. Recognition of the need to look at replication and investment in making it happen are signs of a maturing deployment. A hospitality company found that its early Lean Six Sigma project returns were small because projects were initiated and executed at single locations. However, the savings soon grew a hundred times as the deployment team identified best practices and rolled them out to the whole business.
- *Project tracking.* If a company runs only a handful of projects every year, tracking the investment and the results is relatively simple. But as the deployment matures and interest grows, it becomes more and more important to have a sophisticated system so that deployment leaders can understand the status of all elements of the program.

Component 3: Resources

If you've studied Lean Six Sigma, you know that there are different approaches to staffing the many different deployment positions. Generally, however, companies adopt two strategies, one for staffing the key Lean Six Sigma assignments—Black Belts, Master Black Belts, and deployment champions—and another for filling all of the other roles.

When it comes to the key positions, most organizations today treat them as full- or at least half-time positions, but not on a permanent basis. That is, people give up some or all of their original job responsibilities to rotate into one of the key deployment roles for some period of time. They then move back into line positions. All other participants—sponsors, people serving on just one or two projects, financial representatives helping to validate results, and so on—are generally expected to carry out their Lean Six Sigma responsibilities in addition to doing their regular job.

Early on, particularly in a small, grassroots deployment, the issue of rotating people into and out of the key positions may not be given much consideration, and the talent may be selected based on availability or interest, with little or no effort being made to take advantage of the trained resources after they have completed a project or two. If the deployment process aspires to a higher level of maturity, however, an organization should get more and more sophisticated concerning:

- Who is selected for staff key positions (primarily Black Belts and Master Black Belts), with a trend toward looking for people who are potential leaders in the organization.
- How long (usually 18 months to 2 years for a Black Belt) and to what extent (generally full time, for the best deployments) those people are immersed in Lean Six Sigma work.
- How the resources are integrated (or "repatriated") back into management-track positions after they complete their Lean Six Sigma assignment. More mature deployments recognize that they can get significant benefit by putting people with Lean Six Sigma problem-solving skills into key business roles.

To encourage participation and support not just by the Belts but by all others who participate in the deployment, more mature deployments also start developing reward and recognition programs that acknowledge all contributions to the effort. Lean Six Sigma accomplishments must be seen as something that *everyone* gets credit for, not just the project leader. Companies that recognize only the Black Belt or Green Belt soon see resentment brewing among those who participated but were not acknowledged. Again, as a deployment matures, the organization gets better and better at finding ways to share the recognition. A little can go a long way. Financial awards are used in some companies, but others focus more on nonmonetary forms of recognition, such as a celebratory lunch for the team, a small gift, the opportunity to present results to senior executives, or positive press at departmental events.

Component 4: Training

This is the component that helps you understand how well you are preparing your resources to lead and complete the projects that are priorities for your organization. Seeing the big gains that other organizations have achieved with Lean Six Sigma, some business leaders have become so enthusiastic about getting the same kinds of gains that they have adopted a broad but shallow approach to training: putting masses of people through a standard training program without investing in the rest of the infrastructure or providing the needed project support. Other deployments have gone in the opposite direction, offering training for a minimum number of key personnel and none or very little for others. With experience, however, companies get better at tailoring their training programs so that Black Belts get a broad education suited to the company's needs and other participants get enough training to be able to contribute effectively, but aren't overwhelmed with too much information.

Generally, the key positions (Black Belts, Master Black Belts, and deployment champions) will start out with extensive training on the full DMAIC methodology (Define–Measure–Analyze–Improve–Control), including a combination of Lean and Six Sigma tools and involving work on one or more projects. These people's training needs to include project and change management as well, and may include design methodologies if the design of products or processes is to be part of the implementation.

Another key point is the importance of project coaching to improve learning and accelerate benefits. Coaching bridges the gap between the training and the application of the tools on the projects. A common pitfall occurs when a coach is assigned, but the coach doesn't have the capacity to actually support the projects. Clearly, you will get the benefits of the coaching only if it actually takes place on a regular basis.

As you examine this component to identify improvement opportunities, you will be looking at issues such as who gets trained in what, the kinds of posttraining support offered, and the role of coaching.

Component 5: Culture

As we discussed in Chapter 3, a successful Lean Six Sigma deployment has a two-way relationship with culture: the company has worked to build a culture that is supportive of continuous improvement, but also uses Lean Six Sigma to change the culture in positive ways.

All company cultures are unique and are starting at different places prior to a Lean Six Sigma implementation. In the least mature deployments that we've seen, there is often an attitude in the broader organization that continuous improvement is simply not needed. At the opposite end of the spectrum, Lean Six Sigma is seen as a strategic necessity for keeping the company competitive. You can tell where your company falls along this continuum by looking at attitudes toward issues such as customer focus, prevalence of data-based decision making, the importance of process, and emphasis on continuous improvement.

How to Use a Maturity Model

Now that you have a general sense of what the Lean Six Sigma maturity model looks like, the obvious question is how to put it to use. Most often, a company will bring in an expert or a team of experts in Lean Six Sigma and have those experts evaluate all aspects of the deployment. You have several options on how you choose to approach an evaluation.

Let's look first at whether you should do it yourself or bring in experts. There are two issues at work here:

1. In our experience, the people who are most closely involved in a deployment tend to be a bit rosy in their evaluations, rating it higher or as more mature than it really is. They are also likely to pay the most attention to the aspects of the deployment in which they have been directly involved. Generally, you're better off having your deployment evaluated by someone who is more distant from the day-to-day work because such a person is likely to be more objective and more comprehensive in his efforts. That person could be an expert from a home or central office, someone from another part of your company that is more advanced in its deployment, or a consultant from outside the company.

2. The evaluation is best done by someone who has wide experience with Lean Six Sigma deployments because she will be better able to pick up on signs of struggle or success. If your deployment does not have someone with sufficiently wide experience, it's better to look beyond your borders.

Another factor is whether you should evaluate all the components at once or divide them up. If you use our matrix, there is sufficient detail within each component that you can get useful information by evaluating each one separately. However, most often, the purpose of the assessment is to get an overall view of a deployment and get data that let you compare one component against another—and that means that you should evaluate all the components at the same time.

However you choose to conduct the evaluation, the people involved will use a combination of quantitative data (such as ROI and project cycle times) and subjective measures (such as the quality of the talent in the program) to come up with an overall rating on that component. In situations where subjective information is needed, the deployment team or evaluation experts make their best judgment, perhaps using interviews or internal surveys to gain insights. Either way, the outcome will be an overall rating on each element of the matrix (for a total of 31 scores).

Ideally, your company will have identified target levels in each dimension as well. There is nothing hard and fast about setting targets, although companies will generally aim for at least a Level 3 or Level 4. The effort needed to achieve Level 5 is not always necessary or desirable, given an organization's priorities and resources.

The ratings serve as the starting point for discussions, first among the deployment leadership, and then between them and the company's executive leadership, about where to focus the organization's resources. Again, there are no fixed rules—don't just automatically choose the elements with the lowest scores or those with the largest gap between the actual and desired levels as the first topics to work on. Your leaders need to have a discussion about goals, priorities, and what can realistically be accomplished.

What follows are two case studies to illustrate this process.

Case 1: Using a Maturity Model for an Early-Stage Deployment

We were working with a Fortune 500 manufacturing company that had just started to implement the basics. They had a team of Black

Belts who were working on some successful projects, but the leaders wanted to take the deployment to the next level. By using the maturity model, the company realized that it would need to think more broadly if it were to grow the program to meet the expectations of the business.

The overall scores on their deployment were initially low, but they weren't discouraged. It would be expected to be on the lower end of some of the categories as the program was just getting started. They discussed the results with their leadership and picked a few focus areas to work on.

In particular, the deployment leaders decided to focus on the area of strategic alignment, as they thought that this would produce the most benefit. Figure 6.2 shows both the current-level scores for each element of the strategy section and the desired goal levels.

The maturity model identified a significant gap in strategic alignment, but it also helped the team develop a path forward. For example, the deployment leader was able to attend some upcoming planning meetings for the business and learn more about the business strategy. With this knowledge, the team was able to propose the next round of projects with increased strategic alignment.

Also, the initial program was going reasonably well as a starting point, but the team members knew that return on investment was going to be very important for long-term success and sustainability. As a next step in that direction, they worked with the finance area to identify a financial representative who would support Lean Six Sigma. The financial rep helped them establish metrics and a tracking system. Working with the finance area provided accurate financial measures and also put metrics in place to monitor the overall health of the program.

As the Lean Six Sigma program developed and expanded over the next couple of years, the deployment team continued to revisit the maturity model, scoring their current state and charting their course for the future.

FIGURE 6.2 Evaluation of the strategy section (New deployment)

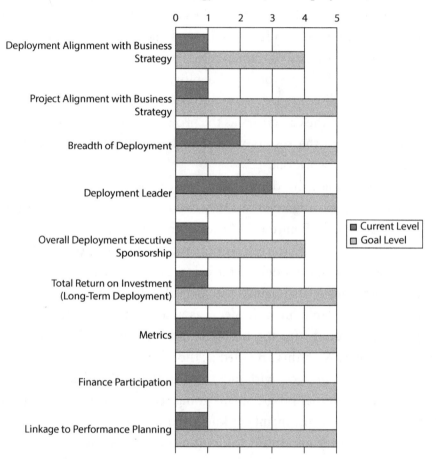

Case 2: Evaluating an Established Deployment

Another Fortune 500 company that we worked with had a mature deployment with high financial returns and significant executive support. They had excellent people in the program and many good projects in process. The leadership team wanted a deployment assessment to identify where the deployment was strong and what opportunities for further development existed. The maturity model helped the company identify some opportunities to make the program even more successful by additionally leveraging some of the grassroots approaches. They decided to take actions to enhance and develop their internal alumni network and become more intentional in terms of support for their Green Belt deployment.

Figure 6.3 shows the results from the project section of the assessment results. As you can see, the overall financial results are great, but there are also some opportunities.

FIGURE **6.3** Evaluation of the project section (Mature deployment)

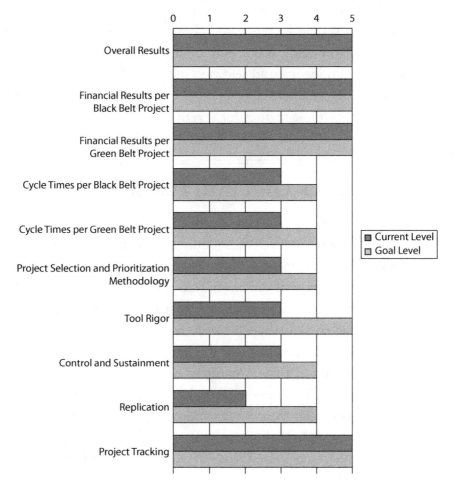

There are two elements here that have a two-point gap between their current and goal levels: replication and tool rigor. As an example of how to address these gaps, the company assigned one of their best Master Black Belts, one who had global experience with the company, to investigate where replication had gone well within the company, identify best practices in those areas, and also look for replication best practices in other companies and industries. The company also made two major changes. First, the deployment team modified the gate review process to specifically address replication, asking questions such as, "How well did this project draw on documented best practices?" and, "What best practices has this project identified that should be replicated elsewhere?" Second, they made the "potential for replication" one of the criteria to be used during project identification and selection meetings. Over the next year, they planned to use their large pool of experienced Green Belts to help with replication activities for several key initiatives.

DEFINING YOUR OWN PATH FORWARD

When you're working in a Lean Six Sigma deployment, it's easy to get consumed by the many details required to keep it on track. Doing an assessment is an effective way to step back from those details and evaluate the overall direction and achievements of a deployment. What we've found in practice is that the assessment has to be detailed enough to define specific steps forward, but not so detailed that it is too complicated or takes too long to complete.

We've also found that a maturity model is a critical tool for executing a Lean Six Sigma assessment. Having a structured tool helps document what your organization thinks is important and helps make sure that nothing critical is missed in the evaluation. Also, being able to compare the observed results against predefined milestones provides an objective way for companies to determine whether they are making sufficient progress.

One last tip: as with the project-selection process we discussed in an earlier chapter, the results of the maturity model ratings should be treated as a starting point for discussions, not a prescription for progress. Having deployment and business leaders discuss the results is the best way to decide how to leverage Lean Six Sigma going forward and make sure that it supports the organization's priorities.

Part 2

Next Steps

The Smart Way to Tackle Bigger Problems, Use More Sophisticated Methods, and Push the Culture to the Next Level

Prologue

What's Next?

Options for Building on a Solid Foundation

In the Tao of Lean Six Sigma, the first part of the path is making sure that there is a good foundation in terms of how the deployment is structured, how it is monitored and managed, and how all the players work together. When the deployment begins to take root and generate successes, the natural question that arises is *what's next?* What can you do to get even more impact? What innovations have leading companies been implementing to take their performance to the next level?

One common answer to that question, and a relatively straightforward next step, is to use the Lean Six Sigma techniques you've mastered in a different part of the business: migrating from manufacturing to service areas, from one plant to multiple plants, or from one department to other departments. If that's what your organization decides to do, our advice is to treat the new application the way you would a new deployment. Revisit the Big Four questions to make sure you know the *why, what, how,* and *who.* Consider whether the messaging and communications from the original deployment area actually fit the new area. Be forewarned that it is seldom possible to copy exactly what you did in one area or application in another area. So while it's a good idea to replicate what works and leverage best practices, be alert for signs that you may need to modify or adapt procedures based on factors like the skill level of the new participants, the types of processes in place, and so forth.

Besides replicating Lean Six Sigma methods in new areas, there are four additional options for taking your initiative to the next level, examples of which are covered in this part of the book:

1. *Get closer to your customers.* The basic DMAIC methodology requires people to understand what customers want and need from a process before they try to improve it, but the simple methodologies can get you only so far. For one thing, they are designed to gather information about customers' reactions to the current version of your product, process, or service—not what unmet needs customers might have that you could solve tomorrow. Neither do they help you balance out competing customer needs (such as lower prices versus improved features). For these and other improvement needs, you need more powerful voice of the customer tools, a handful of which are reviewed in Chapter 7.

2. *Go broader in scope.* One limitation of a traditional project-based Lean Six Sigma approach is that only those people who are directly involved in projects are exposed to improvement thinking and techniques. One way to speed up the gains is to adopt methodologies that are, by design, broader in scope and that involve more pieces of the organization. We've chosen three of the most common and powerful approaches that fit the bill. Business process management (Chapter 8) broadly engages employees and

is a technique for upgrading the performance of the most important processes that cross multiple functions in the organization. Enterprise kaizen (Chapter 9) builds on the basic quick-hit kaizen technique to address businesswide issues. Hoshin planning (Chapter 10) helps ensure that all parts of the business are aligned with strategic priorities, and that those priorities are used to shape improvement efforts.

3. *Target higher levels of performance (getting closer to 6σ).* The discipline of Six Sigma got its name from the concept that a process should have so little variation and such high quality that the yield is 99.99966 percent (that is, there are only about 3 defects per million opportunities). In real life, processes that have not been improved typically operate at abysmal sigma levels, meaning that there is a lot of variation and a lot of defects that increase costs and time. Initial projects using the basic methods and statistical tools can bring that level up to 2σ (69 percent yield) or 3σ (93.3 percent yield), which is adequate in many circumstances. But many business processes can see significant benefits by reducing variation and defects to the point where they achieve much higher sigma levels (4, 5, or even 6). That work requires more sophisticated improvement and analysis tools. Going completely into the details of these methods is beyond the scope of this book, but Chapter 11 previews some of the most useful specialized tools.

4. *Design new products, services, and processes.* The basic Lean Six Sigma methods are great for improving processes that already exist. But to come up with new product or service designs or to significantly rethink a current design, you need methods to gain a deep understanding of customer needs, explore design alternatives, and build

in options for experimentation and testing. Chapter 12 describes the Design for Lean Six Sigma methodology (Define–Measure–Explore–Develop–Implement) that provides the framework for design or redesign projects.

In response to requests that we've received, we have also included a chapter (Chapter 13) that discusses the application of Lean Six Sigma to healthcare organizations. This chapter reviews the similarities and differences between healthcare and other types of organizations, and discusses the special challenges that healthcare organizations face when launching Lean Six Sigma.

7

Voices You *Want* to Hear

Developing Deeper Insights into Customer Needs

WITH MARK SIDOTE

*There is only one boss. The customer. And he can fire
everybody in the company from the chairman on down,
simply by spending his money somewhere else.*
—Sam Walton

How would you measure the customer experience in a fast
food restaurant? A colleague of ours was waiting in line and
observed that the business was measuring the "time from when an
order was placed until the money was collected and the cash register
was closed." This is a reasonable metric for measuring the efficiency
of the cashier. But if the company is interested in improving customer
satisfaction, it will need to track an entirely different and more difficult metric, such as the "time from when a customer gets in line until
he leaves with his purchased food." This second metric reflects the
customer's view of the process—including all the wait times—so it
is a much better indicator of the quality of the customer experience.

This switch from an internal focus to looking at a process
from a customer perspective is familiar to anyone who has worked

with quality improvement disciplines. One of the seminal changes that quality improvement brought to the workplace was a greater emphasis on looking at processes, offerings, and quality through a customer's eyes. "What do our customers want?" is a question that is drilled into quality practitioners.

In fact, building a foundation of basic voice of the customer (VOC) techniques should be a primary emphasis in the initial phases of any Lean Six Sigma deployment (see sidebar). Having a good grasp of internal and external needs is essential for eliminating waste from processes and developing competitive marketplace offerings.

Voice of the Customer Basics

The assumption in this chapter is that you and your organization have already established a foundation of improvement driven by an understanding of your customers and their needs. That would include:

- Identification and segmentation of internal and external customers
- Knowing how to identify what information from customers will help shape improvement or design work
- Being able to differentiate between customer wants and customer needs
- Requiring documentation of customer needs gathered through simple proactive methods (such as surveys and interviews) as well as historical sources (requests, complaints, customer service calls, on-line reviews, and warranty data)

There comes a time, however, when basic techniques cannot provide the deeper insights that help companies surpass customer expectations and provide offerings of compelling value. For that, you need more sophisticated VOC tools. This chapter discusses a sampling of VOC methods that illustrate two major trends that have been adopted by leading companies:

1. Focusing on the customer's experience, not just her stated needs or wants
2. Maintaining strong VOC connections throughout product, process, or service design

Trend 1: Understanding the Customer's Experience

In recent years, organizations have come to realize that customers do not necessarily know or at least cannot easily articulate everything that they are looking for in a product or service. Traditional VOC techniques that rely on customer answers to specific questions are therefore limited in the kinds of insights they can provide. They are best for helping you learn about customer reactions to the features of your current processes or offerings, but they can't help you learn about the needs that customers don't mention or haven't thought about.

That's why there is a new emphasis on VOC methods that help organizations understand how and why customers make the choices they do and what shapes that behavior. There are two components to this trend: first, doing more direct observation of customers, and second, combining multiple sources of data to map out the customer's journey.

Ethnography, Phenomenology, and the Rise of Observational Sciences

You may have heard several new buzzwords in marketing and product design circles in recent years: ethnography and phenomenology. These terms both describe a science based on observations of customers' behavior in their natural habitat, so to speak. By directly observing how customers interact with their environment when they are using a process, product, or service, companies can better understand how and why customers make the decisions they do. This, in turn, leads not just to opportunities to improve the company's existing offerings, but to ways to shape the environment to improve the overall customer experience.

Starbucks, for instance, is famed as a master of phenomenology: studying events from a first-person point of view. From the beginning, the company has focused on increasing profits by not only providing high quality coffee drinks but shaping a particular coffee-drinking experience that historically has allowed them to command premium pricing. Prior to Starbucks, coffee was an inexpensive beverage. Now a coffee shop is a destination for working and meeting friends, with the potential to be a high-margin business.

The story of how Quicken financial software originated is also a story of customer observations. A marketing manager observed his wife's frustration with the boring and repetitive task of paying bills each month. He imagined a computerized software system that would automate the bill-paying process. The other finance products on the market were complicated, targeting financial professionals as their customers. The new product inspired by the marketing manager's wife was designed to look like a checkbook and checkbook register, with simplicity and ease of use as its primary attributes. It quickly became the number one–selling software product in its category. Over time, Quicken continued to listen to its customers and make changes as needed.

To understand the kinds of insights that customer observation can provide, here is a more detailed example. In their 2014 *Harvard Business Review* article, "An Anthropologist Walks into a Bar," authors Christian Madsbjerg and Mikkel Rasmussen describe the experience of a European brewing company that was experiencing falling sales in bars and pubs. When traditional VOC methods failed to help the company determine how to fix the problems, they hired social anthropologists to visit bars and then report their findings. According to the article, the scientists "immersed themselves in the life of the bars, simply observing owners, staff, and regulars" and collected data via videos, still photographs, and field notes.

One insight the brewing company gained from the anthropologists' work was discovering that its ubiquitous promotional materials (coasters, T-shirts, and the like) were largely treated with derision and relegated to storage cabinets or piles of junk. The company immediately scrapped those items (which greatly reduced spending on promotional materials) and developed an entirely new promotional strategy, this time based on training salespeople to work one-on-one with bar owners to develop sales campaigns specific to each bar.

The brewer also discovered that female wait staff—a primary channel for sales—didn't know much about the company's products and didn't want to know more. These staffers were generally resentful of the sexually charged atmosphere in the bars: having to be flirtatious and subject to unwanted advances. As Madsbjerg and Rasmussen report, because of these insights, the company got permission from the bar owners to come in and "create in-workplace 'academies' to train wait staff about its brands." They also won over female servers by providing funds for taxi service for employees who worked late.

As a result of these changes, sales had rebounded within two years—plus the company's market share was showing steady increases.

While this company chose to use professional anthropologists to observe its customers, most companies do not need to go to that extreme. For example, a large manufacturer of home appliances sought to improve sales of its dishwashers by introducing new products. They conducted a series of in-home observational studies of how people interacted with their current dishwashers. From this observation work, they noticed two key improvement themes:

- The person loading the dishwasher felt that he or she had to scrub and prewash all the dishes prior to actually using the dishwasher.
- It was difficult to arrange all the dirty dishes in the space provided. More flexibility was needed.

Additionally, in discussing the dishwasher experience with customers, the team learned that reducing the weekly operating costs by using less water would be desirable, and also that customers liked the trend that new appliances were coming in more colors. By using customer insight to inform the new design from the beginning, the team was able to develop a new product with greater acceptance in the marketplace.

As more and more companies are discovering, there is no substitute for observing customers as they struggle to use a product or service. It can open your eyes in ways you can't anticipate.

Depicting the Full Experience: Customer Journey Maps

Many companies are sitting on a gold mine of customer information, but don't know how to pull it together to get useful insights. One of the best tools for generating a new understanding of customer needs is called a *customer journey map*, also known as a *customer experience map.* Through both words and pictures, this tool captures customers' actions, emotions, concerns, and questions at key points in their interaction with one of your processes or offerings.

A sample customer journey map is shown in Figure 7.1. For this example, we've adopted the viewpoint of a travel reservations company that wants to understand how to make their customer experiences better. They believe that their business will improve not only if customers find their website easy to use, but also if using their services makes the whole travel experience more enjoyable and less stressful.

The start of any customer journey map is deciding on the scope of the investigation. Here, the phases of the travel process—the value streams—are listed in the chevrons across the top (Area 1 in Figure 7.1). The diagram depicts an end-to-end travel experience, so the phases cover everything from planning and researching to writing reviews after the event. If you were studying the customer experience associated with a product, the diagram might cover everything from purchase to installation, support, service, and replacement. Or the scope might be much narrower if you were looking at just one aspect of a product or service.

The second part of the map (Area 2) shows the actions that customers take, and, most important, the touch points that they have with any product or service provider. As you can see in the example, the key is to capture the touch points in pictures, not just words. The visual component is crucial because you want the basic flow of the process and the touch points to be easily understood by anyone who looks at the map. (This version uses simple icons that are available on the web to illustrate the customer's actions, but you can use any kind of pictures.)

The last part of the diagram (the customer thoughts section, Area 3) is where customer journey maps are differentiated from any

FIGURE 7.1 Customer journey map for a travel experience

Journey	Research & Planning	Shopping	Booking / Post-Booking	Travel	Posttravel
Actions	Research destinations, travel products & services	Enter destinations/dates; Review prices; Select products	Review itinerary; Confirm itinerary; Review payment options; Confirm payment; Receive itinerary; Change plans	Have fun; Write reviews	Share experience; Plan next trip

Gather Information

Destinations
Friends / Co-workers
Chat with Travel Professional
Talk with Travel Professional
Travel sites, hotels, blogs, etc.

Customer
Itinerary
Change/Cancel plans
Call for help with complex itinerary

Share Photos

Thoughts

- Where should I go on my vacation?
- What are my options?
- How much will it cost?
- What are some of the attractions?
- Where will I stay?
- How will I get there?
- Are there any low-cost options?
- Can I use reward points?
- Will I need a car?
- What travel documents are required?
- How long is the flight?
- What is the weather this time of year?
- What currency is needed?
- What is the exchange rate?

- My plans are complex. I may need help.
- What is the change fee?
- What if my itinerary is incorrect?
- Is the price the same as I was quoted?
- Can I add another two days to my trip?
- What happens if I have to cancel my trip? Will I get my money back?
- Can I purchase travel insurance? How much will it cost?

- Where is my gate?
- What if my bags don't arrive?
- I can't wait to show my photos to my friends and family.
- Where should I travel to next?
- How can I write a review for the hotel, airline, cruise, etc.?

other kind of process map. Knowing what customers need and how they feel during each phase and touch point can help companies deliver that exceptional experience.

To develop this part of the map, you would start with a review of all the customer information you already have. Most companies today capture an array of analytics through various listening posts: information concerning web pages visited, online reviews, complaints, customer service logs, lost customers, returns, and many others. Data mining this information can be a great start in understanding your customers' needs. You might also have notes from interviews, surveys, or observations of customers as they interact with your products and services in their native environment; if you don't, consider collecting this kind of information as well.

Use the information to help you answer key questions about each step, such as:

- What are customers doing at each point in the process? What would they like to be doing?
- What problems are they experiencing or could they be experiencing?
- How are the customers' needs being addressed?
- Do the customers have any concerns about how your company is meeting their needs during this step? How else might you attend to their needs?

Any statements that are linked to these questions are what you would put into the "customer thoughts" section of the customer journey map.

By combining these elements, you get a quick picture of what it's like for the customer to use your product or service in the fuller context of everything that has to happen if this customer is to achieve a desired outcome.

The map in Figure 7.1, for example, summarizes a lot of information:

- The key actions that the customer takes, from researching and planning a trip, to shopping for the best deals and booking the trip, to actually traveling and then sharing their experiences after they return
- The touch points where the customer interacts with the travel site's services or other services (using websites, talking to travel professionals, calling customer service to change plans, or interacting with multiple service providers)
- Key concerns that occupy customers' minds as they engage the travel service company

By analyzing these data, the travel services company could look at ways to ensure that customer concerns are addressed during the touch points where the customer is interacting with the company. That might include having liberal cancellation policies and making it easy for customers to figure out how to use rewards points or to change plans. The company could also look at ways to improve the overall travel experience. This way, customers will continue to use the site not just for the ease of booking, but also because they are confident that they can trust the information they receive in making decisions about destinations, accommodations, and attractions.

Bonus Example: Insulation Industry Customer Journey Map

A company was interested in creating a new spray-applied insulation product for the housing market. They looked at the entire end-to-end process to understand how the current products on the market were being experienced by contractors and homeowners. They realized that the installer's experience was the key to sales because the contractors had significant influence over the buying decision. The homeowner was interested in basic information about the performance and quality of the product, but was largely indifferent to small variations between brands.

Based on observations and a series of interviews, the company determined that significant innovation was needed in application and installation. Many opportunities were identified, but the most significant was that the existing products took too long to dry. This created a hassle for the contractor and added significant expense for both the contractor and the homeowner.

To address this customer concern, a product team designed and developed completely new application equipment along with a new process for installing the insulation. With the new product, contractors were able to apply the insulation in hours instead of a full day, which completely changed their experience with the product and significantly increased their productivity and revenue. The new product also provided a cost reduction to the homeowner and increased the insulation company's market share.

As with many tools, the value of a customer journey map lies as much in the work used to create it as in the final product. Looking at a process through your customers' eyes and understanding their thoughts, feelings, and emotions along the way can uncover a wealth of opportunities that may otherwise go unnoticed. Since customer journey maps help capture that information, one of their main uses is to help focus design, development, and improvement efforts. Uncovering those "aha" moments helps the design or improvement teams deliver a superior customer experience.

TREND 2: MAINTAINING STRONG VOC THROUGHOUT THE DESIGN PROCESS

In any design project—be it for a product, a service, a process, or some combination of the three—teams face countless decisions that require precision and an understanding of trade-offs. A general understanding of customer needs is of little use in these situations. It's not enough to know, for example, that customers want "quick turnaround." You need to know whether that means instantaneous service or service in an hour, a day, or a week—and what the customer is willing to pay for different levels of service. He may want a one-hour turnaround but only be willing to pay enough to support a one-day turnaround.

Being able to connect front-end VOC information with design and development decisions is another way in which companies are working to get more value out of the VOC information that they collect. Here, we focus on two methods that play a key role in fulfilling this need: quality function deployment (also known as the House of Quality) and conjoint analysis.

Involving Customers in the Design Process

In recent years, fans of high-end cars have been excited about participating in the design of several Porsche automobiles.

The first came when the carmaker had reached 2 million Facebook fans, and the second was released at the 5-million-fan milestone.

The design for the "5 Million Porsche Fans" car was shaped by votes from 54,000 fans. The one-of-a-kind car was unveiled in August 2013, sporting exclusive deep-blue paintwork, special wheels, aerodynamic features, and a 3.8-liter six-cylinder boxer engine with 430 hp. You can't buy this car, but customers can get behind the wheel at Porsche's driving school in England.

While the custom-designed Porsche cars have not yet affected the underlying design concepts that the company uses, the efforts indicate the enormous interest that companies have in getting their customers engaged in the design process, and the design input may be used in the future.

Quality Function Deployment (QFD)

Suppose you wanted to design a process for delivering a perfect cup of coffee. If you ask coffee drinkers about their needs, "hot coffee" will probably be near the top of the list. That's a good starting point, but what does "hot" mean? The average customer could not tell you in degrees what temperature would meet that requirement—she just knows that she doesn't want either cold coffee or something so hot that it burns her mouth. However, this more detailed information would be needed to create the ideal coffee-drinking experience, so you conduct a little research and come up with the answers shown in Figure 7.2. With this information, you can then decide how to set the temperatures on the coffee machine so that by the time the customer receives her coffee, its temperature is approximately 77°C.

FIGURE 7.2 Moving from customer needs to specific requirements

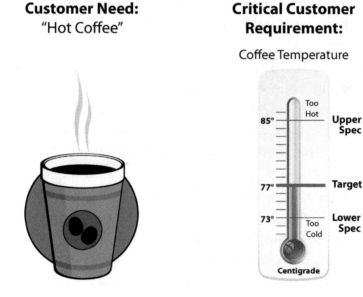

Customer Need:
"Hot Coffee"

Critical Customer Requirement:

Coffee Temperature

This simple example illustrates the purpose of quality function deployment (QFD): to turn general statements of customer needs into information that can be used to make decisions about the design, manufacture, and delivery of a process, product, or service. In that way, QFD creates a much-needed bridge between marketing, design, and engineering.

To facilitate this translation, QFD relies on a diagram known as the House of Quality (Figure 7.3).

As you can see in the figure, we begin with the customer needs, expressed as they were heard from the customers (Area 1). These needs are gathered directly from customer interactions and are weighted based on their importance to the customer. Across the top of the matrix (Area 2) are the critical customer requirements (CCRs), or how the design team is going to measure to what extent the design has met the customer needs. The strength of the relationship

FIGURE **7.3** House of quality

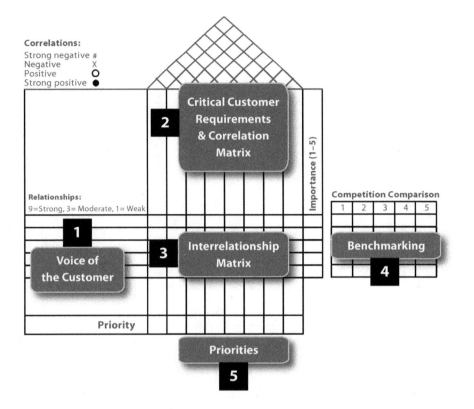

between the critical customer requirements and the customer needs is determined (Area 3), and the weighted sum of these results sets the overall priority (Area 5). A good House of Quality also captures information that shows how your company compares to others in your industry in meeting the customer needs (Benchmarking, Area 4). The other areas are used to evaluate the relationships between and within these factors.

A simplified House of Quality is shown in Figure 7.4. This diagram was developed as part of a project to design a new piece of construction equipment. Details are described in the figure caption.

FIGURE 7.4 QFD example

In this example of construction equipment design, the customer needs show that customers want the machine to be quiet, sufficiently fast, and easy to service. This translated into CCRs related to technical issues such as roading speed, ambient sound, and frequency of dealer repair. Here, the serviceability index scores the highest overall, as this critical customer requirement is strongly related to two customer needs and either moderately or slightly related to two others. The competition comparison tells us that the existing product is mostly average, but has good cab access and poor fuel capacity compared with the top two competitors.

Correlations:
Strong negative #
Negative ×
Positive ○
Strong positive ●

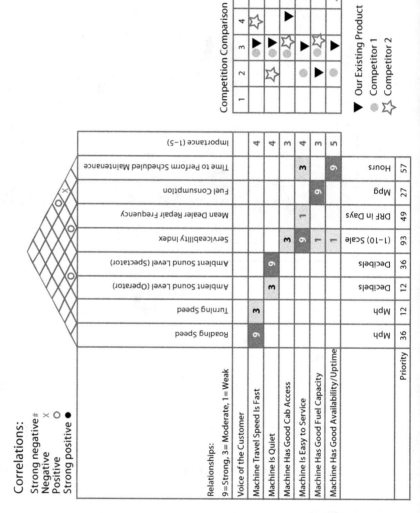

While conducting a QFD analysis adds some time to the front-end phases of a design project, it shortens the overall time because all the players involved in designing and delivering the offering are on the same page from the start. QFD roots all discussions in the quantification and documentation of customer needs. In completing this diagram, the players can have discussions about design features and trade-offs early on, when the elements are still fluid and can be easily (and inexpensively) changed. That improves team alignment from the beginning, reducing the number of disagreements that typically arise down the road and avoiding time-consuming and expensive rework.

Conjoint Analysis: Balancing "Wants" with the Willingness to Pay

For many years, designers and engineers have known that there is a big difference between asking customers, "Would you like this new feature in our offering?" and asking them, "Would you be willing to pay $X to add this feature to our offering?" Customers will say that they want nearly everything (preferably "yesterday" and "for free"), but you get a very different picture if you ask them how much they would be willing to pay. The same goes if you ask them about their priorities; maybe they want both quality and speed, but for a particular price, they would place a higher emphasis on quality.

In addition, asking customers about features and pricing as isolated factors is a dangerous path. Customers don't think about features separately from one another; they are looking at the total package of what you have to offer.

Being able to evaluate multiple and often contradictory customer needs is where conjoint analysis comes in. It allows you to get customer reactions to different combinations of features and pricing, so that you can evaluate priorities and better understand what customers are and are not willing to pay for.

Here's an example of how conjoint analysis works. An international hotel chain wanted to understand more about their brand, key price points, and the value of their loyalty program. They were wondering whether customers would pay more per night for a stay in their hotel than they would for a room at their biggest competitor's hotel (a comparison that is typically hard to quantify). They also wanted to test price sensitivity and get input on their loyalty program. So the hotel presented customers with a number of scenarios that reflected different combinations of these features (a higher rate with the same loyalty program, a higher rate with a better loyalty program, and so on).

The results were a mix of good news and bad news:

- Bad news: There was no statistical difference in the value of the brands. Customers would not be willing to pay more for a stay at this hotel than for a stay at the competing brand.
- Good news: Customers seemed insensitive to a slight price increase, so the company could increase rates a little without risk of losing their customer base. (The company then began a second round of study to identify exactly where the price points were.)
- Bad and good news: Improving its loyalty program would *not* increase repeat customer business, but removing it altogether would have a significant negative impact. The bad news, therefore, was that the company could not use its loyalty program to increase business and would have to look for other strategies for increasing customer retention. The good news, however, was that the company could just maintain its current loyalty program.

This ability to evaluate multiple features and pricing alternatives is one of the most attractive features of conjoint analysis. In particular, those companies whose products or services are Internet-based can use conjoint analysis quite easily because they can mock up the different scenarios to get feedback from customers. For example:

- A financial services company wanted to improve efficiencies in the process for updating account information. The conjoint analysis presented customers with two web options for each key step in the process. From the analysis, the team determined which steps were important to customers and the preferred web format for those steps.
- A pharmaceutical company wanted to gather customer insight on their website as part of a redesign and rebranding effort. They tested putting important information in various locations to optimize ease of use. They also looked at different color schemes, menu orientations, and graphics. As a result of the experiment, they determined which design the customers preferred, and were also able to collect data about which websites the customers were able to navigate the most quickly.

THE CHALLENGE OF UNDERSTANDING CUSTOMERS

If I had asked people what they wanted, they would have said faster horses.
—*Henry Ford*

We know from our experience that it can be difficult to gain a deep understanding of the voice of the customer. Today, that goal is being achieved by leading companies in two primary ways:

- First, companies today know that they need to incorporate data collection methods that let them go beyond hearing the "customer's voice" to understanding needs that customers cannot articulate. They are turning to methods like observation and customer journey maps to develop deeper insights concerning how to shape and improve the customer's experience.

● Second, the companies that are leading the charge in product and service design know that merely understanding customer needs is of limited use. They need tools that can help them translate imprecise, fuzzy customer statements into information that they can use to make specific and often technical decisions about the design and operation of processes, products, and services.

If your company has established a good foundation with basic VOC techniques, we highly recommend that you experiment with customer observation. Get out into your customer's environment and simply watch as he performs the function or conducts the work that involves your product or service. You'll be amazed at what you can learn.

To get more out of your customer information, look to the more sophisticated VOC tools. We highlighted just three in this chapter (customer journey maps, quality function deployment, and conjoint analysis), but there are many others that you can use. Depending on the level of training among your Black Belts and Master Black Belts, you may already have the internal expertise you need to start using these tools on design and process improvement projects.

8

Business Process Management

Building a Strong Foundation for Implementing a Culture of Improvement

In just five years, a start-up services company had grown 100-fold, from having only 120 employees to having more than 12,000 employees. The pressure was tremendous to develop a mechanism so that work that had previously been handled by one or two people could be completed accurately by multiple work groups across diverse geographies. Also, the industry was increasingly regulated, and the company needed to be confident that it could document its compliance and meet the required standards.

The challenge this company faced didn't fall into the traditional focus of Lean Six Sigma: fixing problems or making improvements. Its need was much more fundamental: simply being able to get work done quickly and reliably. The company's leaders wanted a way to help them create and maintain sound business practices during a time of rapid growth.

Consider another situation, involving a much older multibillion-dollar corporation with three times as many employees. A global leader in its industry, the corporation had been using Lean Six Sigma for many years, and had made countless improvements generating millions of dollars in benefits. It had a very stable organizational structure and a well-established improvement infrastructure. However, an assessment revealed that there was a weak spot: improvement efforts often struggled with sustainment and control, getting changes to stick once they were in place.

Despite the obvious differences, these two situations had a similar core problem: a lack of process mastery. Both organizations were hindered because they had not put sufficient effort into understanding and managing the processes used to do the work of the business. The solution for both was also the same: business process management (BPM).

Use of BPM is still something of a frontier because it is not nearly as widely used as it could be. In fact, if you ask a dozen people what BPM is, you're likely to hear a dozen different answers. Most people will have a vague notion that it is some kind of management discipline that has something to do with process improvement. Some will think that it's a technology for process documentation. Others will see it as a way to use software to model and automate business processes. Still others may think of it as a dumbed-down version of Lean Six Sigma.

While all of these definitions contain a kernel of truth, none of them captures the true power and impact of this methodology. BPM provides the tools that every business needs if it is to manage its critical processes—the ones it relies on to thrive in the marketplace—in a way that ensures high performance. With BPM, organizations are able to standardize, document, and control how work gets done. That makes their critical functions more reliable and often confers higher levels of productivity.

In short, the process mastery created by a solid BPM program builds a strong foundation that helps organizations achieve their strategic goals, conquer operational challenges, and better leverage previously established improvement efforts. For these reasons, we strongly believe that BPM should be a part of every organization's arsenal of management disciplines.

One of the biggest benefits of BPM is getting basic process tools into the hands of the people who manage and operate the process on a daily basis, not just the people who are involved in an improvement effort. This facilitates a broader culture of continuous improvement and empowers employees across the organization.

In this chapter, we'll talk about the components of the BPM methodology and how to make it successful in any organization.

THE STARTING POINT: CRITICAL PROCESSES

Every organization gets work done through processes large and small. Putting a significant amount of effort into documenting and managing all of those processes would take years, and the overall payoff might not be worth the effort. That's why, just as with any initiative, you need to focus BPM efforts on those areas that will generate the biggest payback.

Typically, a BPM initiative will be launched by a designated team of people, just as you would do with a Lean Six Sigma deployment. One of the first tasks of the BPM team is to identify the organization's *critical processes*, those related to the organization's ability to compete and win in its chosen markets, plus any that have been identified by the top leadership as essential to achieving strategic priorities.

As shown in Figure 8.1, critical processes can be *core processes*, those that deliver value to the customer, or *support processes*, those processes that are needed to keep a business operational.

FIGURE 8.1 Core and support processes

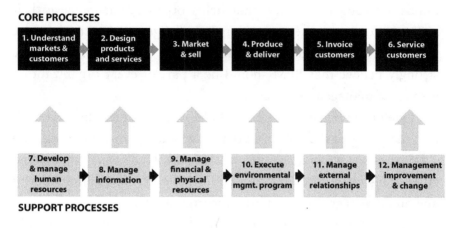

Here are some examples of critical processes targeted by BPM:

- *Any part of the value chain that is contributing to customer dissatisfaction.* Finding and fixing processes that contribute to unhappy customers is often the initial target for a BPM effort. For a service organization, that would mean looking at portions of the value chain that take too long or do not meet customer needs. One service company, for example, chose to focus on post-sales support as the starting point of an initiative to increase customer satisfaction.
- *Any core process that is related to a strategic goal.* If an organization needs to focus on, say, cost reduction or growth, the target would be to manage processes that have high costs or those that enable growth. One company that set an aggressive strategic goal for growth realized that it was critical that they manage their new product development process more actively, so that they could get new products out to the market more quickly.
- *Any support process that is tied to a strategic goal.* Many companies have strategic goals that require their support

processes to function more effectively. For example, companies in industries with a shortage of talent know that support processes such as hiring and onboarding can be critical because they need to be able to attract, quickly hire, and retain top talent. There are other companies where initiatives such as "going green" have been identified as priorities, in which case any processes with an environmental impact would be considered critical.

Tying BPM to processes linked to the company's strategic issues is critical to delivering the kind of payback that a business needs from such an investment.

THREE PHASES OF PROCESS MANAGEMENT

Once the critical processes are defined, the next step is to begin actively managing them. While the definitions of BPM vary from source to source, there is general agreement that process management encompasses three phases: *defining*, *measuring*, and *controlling* a process. The tools used to carry out these functions will sound familiar to anyone who has experience with Lean or Six Sigma. Figure 8.2 shows a summary of tools and methods by phase; more detail follows.

Define the Process

The purpose of this step is to understand and document the process of interest from both a process and a customer perspective. The first step is often creating a SIPOC diagram—a high-level process map that identifies the major components of the process: Suppliers, Inputs, Process steps, Outputs, and Customers. The goal at this point is to create a high-level view of the key process elements in a single,

FIGURE 8.2 Process management steps and tools

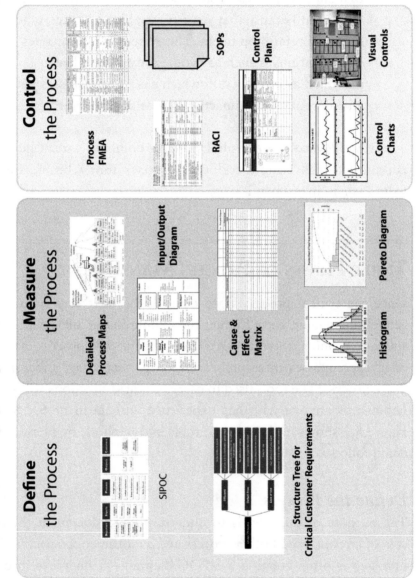

simple diagram that can be used to align everyone around the process boundaries and elements. The team will dive down into detail in the next phase.

In developing the SIPOC diagram, the team will identify the major customers of the process and document those customers' needs. Customer needs are often well known from existing surveys or interviews, and that existing information can be used to verify those needs. If there are no or only limited customer needs data, the team will have to collect additional information:

- If the process has an internal customer, identifying needs is usually just a matter of bringing together a few key employees—the process owner, some process subject matter experts, and the process customer—for a brainstorming session. The identified needs are organized using an affinity diagram and then summarized with an appropriate tool, such as a structure tree diagram, that shows the links between needs and specific, measurable critical customer requirements (CCRs).

- If the process delivers a product or service to an external customer, the methods for gathering voice of the customer (VOC) data can be much more elaborate, especially if the process is new or under development. (See Chapter 7 for an overview of VOC methods.) However, even if you have existing VOC data on the relevant customers, it might be good to gather new data (do a VOC refresh), particularly if you're seeing customer complaints about the targeted process. If the current process is having significant difficulty meeting customer needs, that is an indicator that process improvement is needed, and you may prefer to launch a full DMAIC project for this process.

Measure the Process

The Measure phase establishes how the process operates and performs today. This phase benefits from the use of common process-mapping techniques to document the process as it currently exists, help identify useful metrics for the process, and establish a standard document for communicating information about the process. Typically, the BPM team will use one or more of the following types of process maps:

- *Value stream map (VSM).* In simplest terms, a value stream map is a process map with data. The map shows the high-level steps of the process (with slightly more detail than the P in the SIPOC map) and includes key performance data. An initial value stream map can typically be created by a team within a few hours. However, identifying and gathering the data may take longer, depending on the current data collection systems. Manufacturing processes will often have more readily available data than service or transactional processes, but VSMs can be constructed for any type of process.

- *Cross-functional process maps.* These maps are typically used to show more detail concerning the steps in a process, including detail about decision points and handoffs between people or groups. This makes them particularly useful for documenting transactional processes that have multiple handoffs between departments and are prone to rework loops. Cross-functional maps are typically developed at one level down from the steps identified in the SIPOC map. A good rule of thumb for process map detail is that as you go down a level, you should describe the top-level step in five to seven more detailed steps. In this way, a five- to seven-step SIPOC-level map becomes a 25- to 49-step detailed process map. You can continue diving down as needed if your process needs more detail to be understood.

- *Input/output maps.* These show the detailed inputs and outputs of each process step, which are helpful in identifying potential input variables that have large effects on your output measures. The inputs feed the cause-and-effect matrix, which helps you prioritize what you need to measure going forward.

In documenting the critical process, the BPM team should identify which inputs may potentially have the biggest impact on the process outputs and which steps require more data collection to better understand the causes, problems, or relationships between factors. They can use a variety of simple graphical and data analysis tools (such as Pareto charts) to perform any needed analysis. This work will help the team understand at a deeper level what is actually happening and what kind of performance is being achieved.

Control the Process

In the Control phase, the BPM team documents standard operating procedures and establishes ownership of the different tasks in the process. The team members will also identify high-risk areas and develop control plans for reacting to signs of trouble. The team also has the responsibility for making sure that everyone who is working with the process has the knowledge and tools to perform the work correctly.

Many tools are available to manage the process once it is documented. Most groups will want to use charts that help establish responsibilities around the process (such as a RACI chart) and have documented standard operating procedures (SOPs).

Some groups may want to have clearly documented plans for responding to problems [for example, with process failure mode and effects analysis (FMEA) charts]. Most groups will benefit from using visual controls that allow the process workers to clearly understand what they are supposed to do and quickly identify when the process has gone off course. The more visual the tools, the more likely it is that people will use them.

The process owners should continue to review the key process measures as dictated by the control plan. Ideally, they will monitor the data on a control chart (or other appropriate chart, depending on the type of data). This monitoring involves a bit of work at first to get the appropriate systems set up, but over time, the overall burden on the process owners should be small once they get comfortable with the metrics. They will gradually get better at knowing when a problem is significant (and therefore requires a response) and when it is incidental (meaning that it is a typical part of the process fluctuations).

Software Comes *After* Documentation

As you may have noticed in this section, there is no special software that is essential to business process management. Many companies have gained great benefit from BPM without having a central repository or other functions provided by specialized software.

However, some organizations may find it helpful to use software to store the process documentation centrally, have the ability to link the documents and the measures, or help model variations in the process operations. If those functionalities would help your company, we advise you to consider your software options *after* you have your processes under control; you'll make a better decision about whether to use software and what package is best once you fully understand your process management needs.

Companies that reverse that advice—that get the software first and then start working on BPM—often pay a steep price. Some companies have invested millions of dollars up front, only to realize after they launched the BPM methodology that the software didn't provide the capabilities that they really needed.

Process Management Summary

In each of the phases of process management—defining, measuring, and controlling—the focus should be on using the best tools possible to allow people to document process steps and gather and analyze data in order to understand and manage the process. Above all, adopt a Lean mentality in this area: if the tool or documentation does not provide value, it is waste. Every organization will need to define for itself the minimum set of documents that should be used in each phase, make sure that people are trained in how to use them, and update those tools as necessary.

IMPLEMENTATION

Incorporating BPM into an organization is relatively straightforward. The company needs to identify the people who are responsible for the critical processes it has selected—including the identification of a process owner for each process (see sidebar)—train those people in the necessary BPM tools, and then establish new routines that require ongoing updates to BPM documents and data monitoring.

What Is a Process Owner?

The process owner has responsibility for ensuring that the process meets key performance metrics and is satisfying the customer requirements in an efficient and effective manner. Ideally, the participants in the process all report directly to the process owner. For example, the director of human resources is likely to be the process owner for the hiring and onboarding processes, and the staff members supporting these processes usually report to him.

No matter what pathway you choose, the goal is to get the process owners (and other process participants as needed) truly engaged in managing their own processes. The options for achieving this goal are many. Here are two typical pathways:

- If you have an established team of Black Belts associated with Lean Six Sigma, you can leverage their expertise. Select some of them to study your organization and develop recommendations around what critical processes should be tackled first. They can then work with process owners to develop the documentation and metrics needed for BPM, and teach the process owners on the go as the work is completed.
- An alternative is to develop the equivalent of a Yellow Belt team in a Lean Six Sigma program by providing focused training on BPM to selected resources, most likely the process owners. In this approach, the process owners would receive perhaps a day of training on the

Define and Measure phases, then have several months
on their own to identify core measures and complete the
documentation of process steps. They would then return
to the classroom for a second day of training on Control,
and then follow up by completing the necessary process
documents. The benefit of this approach is that the process
owners learn the tools and establish new habits for
managing their processes.

Once the training is complete and the BPM documentation and
monitoring systems are in place, the focus shifts to sustainment,
which includes ongoing monitoring and operations, identifying
potential improvement projects, and occasionally updating the documentation as the process changes.

The resource requirements and overall timeline for developing
and implementing BPM practices will vary considerably depending on what resources and knowledge each organization has available and the commitment levels of its process owners. Typically,
the initial round of documentation can be completed within two
months of starting the project (assuming that a team meets for
several hours a week). We've also seen some companies complete
this work significantly faster—within a one-week kaizen format.
In a BPM kaizen event, the team works together for a few days or
a week, concentrating solely on the BPM deliverables. While this
approach requires the team members to block their schedules for
a period of time, the overall time commitment is smaller, the deliverables are completed sooner, and the team typically has a positive
experience.

Example Rollout

To maintain control over its operations under conditions of such
rapid growth and regulatory pressure, the company introduced at

the beginning of this chapter identified 10 critical processes, including forecasting, sales, purchasing, contracting, payments, modeling, services delivery, and equities trading. They then identified a single point of responsibility—a process owner—for each process and key subprocesses. Additionally, they identified key metrics to measure the performance of each of those processes.

They then developed a two-day BPM curriculum that covered topics spanning all three phases in the BPM road map (Define, Measure, and Control). The company trained approximately a hundred staff members, all of whom had control over some part of the 10 critical processes and related subprocesses. Within two months of the training, each person had to produce a full set of BPM deliverables, including a SIPOC diagram, critical customer requirements, a detailed process map, and a control plan.

Gradually, over the next year, all 10 critical processes were completely documented, with process owners in place and a plan for ongoing measurement. As a consequence, the organization found it easier to deal with its continued expansion, since each new operation could either use BPM to develop its own standard operating procedures or draw on existing standards elsewhere in the company. As its BPM practices took hold, customer satisfaction increased, average process cycle times went down, and regulatory compliance was improved significantly.

INTEGRATING BPM INTO AN ORGANIZATION

As demonstrated by the experience of the rapidly growing company just discussed, which did not have any prior experience with Lean or Six Sigma, BPM can be launched as a stand-alone initiative. Their effort was implemented solely to get critical processes well documented and well managed. More often, however, BPM is used to complement existing improvement and/or design efforts. Here is one example.

A financial services company had an evolving process improvement initiative, starting with total quality management (TQM) methods a decade ago and building into a Lean Six Sigma program. But they found that they were struggling with Lean Six Sigma because of a lack of process ownership, lack of clearly defined processes, and lack of process management. This made it hard for the company to identify opportunities before projects were launched and more difficult for it to get a handle on implementing and sustaining improvements at project completion.

To overcome these issues, the company decided to make basic BPM training a prerequisite for any employee who was going to attend Lean Six Sigma courses. The attendees had to identify a critical process and produce the BPM deliverables within six months of completing the class. When they later attended Lean or Six Sigma training, they had to bring the BPM documentation of the process that was being targeted—meaning that they showed up for the more advanced training with a clear process owner already identified and in place, the "as-is" process already documented, and the current process performance well understood. Having all this basic information available helped them significantly shorten the cycle time to achieve process improvements.

One way to view BPM's purpose in an organization is shown in Figure 8.3. Meeting the strategic objectives for any business (top of the triangle) is likely to require some combination of managing critical processes better (the core of the triangle), improving existing processes (the left side of the triangle), and designing new processes (the right side of the triangle). While many organizations already have process improvement efforts, fewer have developed a robust process design capability (discussed in Chapter 12) or have integrated BPM into their day-to-day process management routines.

FIGURE 8.3 Where BPM fits in

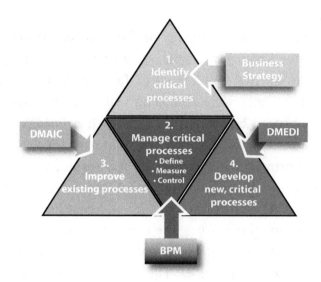

Although the figure shows process improvement, process management, and process design as three separate entities, in real life there is a great deal of overlap among the three. For example, many tools within the process improvement (DMAIC) and process design (DMEDI) road maps are focused on understanding and documenting the process. Those same tools are at the heart of BPM, as we discussed earlier in this chapter. Because of this overlap, organizations that are already involved in improvement or process design are likely to have basic competence in the BPM tools, and vice versa.

There are other ways in which the methods complement one another. Here are two of the most important.

Becoming a Springboard for Identifying Improvement Projects

The focus of BPM is on controlling and managing processes as they exist today. However, the up-front work needed to document processes as part of a BPM program will undoubtedly identify many areas that could use improvement or expose gaps where new processes need to be designed. Similarly, ongoing BPM activities—such as monitoring key metrics—will also help bring potential improvement areas to the surface and alert the organization's leaders when critical processes are not meeting performance goals. In short, BPM is a great engine for generating process improvement and process design ideas.

The key is to pair BPM's idea-generation capability with project selection and chartering activities. As we discussed in Chapter 5 on project selection, having a hopper of vetted ideas is a critical step in project pipeline management. All you'll need is a mechanism for feeding those ideas into the evaluation and prioritization steps. When you make this connection, you'll have a supply of prioritized projects, linked to critical processes, that can be used when you have the resources to run a Black Belt, Green Belt, or kaizen project.

Maximizing the Effectiveness of the Control Phase of DMAIC

The larger company that we discussed earlier already had a long-standing Lean Six Sigma program. But since they struggled with control and sustainment, they implemented BPM to develop more process awareness and ownership throughout the organization. As they learned, Black Belt projects executed within critical processes that were part of a BPM initiative had much more successful hand-offs because there was an established process owner in place who was already using the kinds of process control and management tools needed to maintain the gains. Over time, more and more processes were assigned process owners and more BPM techniques were established. Because of this, the improvements developed by DMAIC teams were also implemented, controlled, and sustained more successfully. Lean Six Sigma project cycle times were also significantly reduced, since so much foundational work had been completed in advance.

Keys to BPM Success

Different companies are at different levels of process maturity. Wherever you are on your journey, the keys to successful BPM implementation include:

- A focus on critical processes that are linked to strategic business priorities and are actively supported at the executive level
- Use of a very basic suite of tools to manage and measure process performance and to ensure that processes perform at a consistently high level
- Use of the BPM efforts to feed priority projects into the improvement pipeline

It takes hard work and continued effort for companies to get a good return on their BPM investment, but the benefits are huge. They include the confidence that comes from knowing that the most important processes in your organization are going to perform reliably and that your employees are empowered with the knowledge and tools they need to continue to improve the processes they use every day.

9

Quick Fixes for Big Issues: Enterprise kaizen

WITH CHUCK COX

A rapidly growing international company with nearly 60,000 employees working in 80 countries was having trouble filling all of its new job openings for technical positions. The company spent a great deal of time finding ideal candidates. On average, it took well over three months for the hiring process to reach a point where the company could make a firm offer. During those months, however, the recruits would often be poached by competing companies that were willing to make a job offer within three or four weeks. That left the international company scrambling, having to start the hiring process all over again.

To solve this problem, the company charged two directors with the task of overhauling their two pieces of the company's human resources (HR) processes. The directors were given six months to complete a Lean Six Sigma project targeted at slashing the hiring timeline by about 50 percent (to less than two months on average).

If you have any experience with changing large organizational silos, you know that a six-month timeline is extremely ambitious for such a significant change. In fact, once we got a good look at their processes, we realized the situation was even worse. It was clear to us that this company simply could not reach its cycle-time goal by changing just the two core processes controlled by the two directors. The HR hiring processes crossed four silos, not just two, and the company would need to improve all four major parts of the HR system in order to get a process that reached the two-month cycle-time target. It was clear that no matter how fast the processes controlled by the two directors became, the overall hiring process would take longer than two months because of speed constraints in the other two areas.

That realization led us to develop two options for this company. They could stick with a traditional Lean Six Sigma project timeline, where the two directors and a core team met weekly to work on the processes. Under this approach, a realistic deadline for reaching the target improvement would be 12 months, not six. Or they could use a different approach called enterprise kaizen that would require them to bring all the players (about 55 people from around the globe) together in the same location for a full week, but would generate the result that they wanted within the six-month targeted time frame.

The company resisted this advice for some time. The VP of human resources thought it was impractical to allocate so many resources to the enterprise kaizen for a full week.

However, because filling these technical positions was so important to the company's strategy, the VP ultimately decided that he was more reluctant to extend the timeline to 12 months and would rather try the enterprise kaizen approach, which he didn't know much about. By way of a spoiler, we'll tell you that the company succeeded in reaching the less than two-month cycle time target for its HR processes within the six-month deadline.

But first, we'll talk about the enterprise kaizen approach, which is based on the kaizen event model that is commonly used in Lean projects. If you're already familiar with the kaizen event model, you can skip the next section and go right to the enterprise kaizen overview.

KAIZEN EVENTS: ONE-WEEK WONDERS

The standard project model used in Lean or Six Sigma (and most other improvement approaches) is to establish a project team that meets for a couple of hours a couple of times per week over a period of four to six months until a problem is solved and the solution is implemented.

In contrast, a kaizen improvement project is treated more like an event. A carefully selected group of people comes together (most often physically, not just virtually) and works exclusively on the problem for about one work week. The event leaders need to do some up-front prep work and follow-on implementation work, so the total cycle time is more like a month to six weeks, but the bulk of the improvement thinking and project work occurs during that single event week.

Because a lot has to happen in such a concentrated period, kaizen events have historically been launched to tackle very focused issues involving improving process speed and reducing waste. By "focused," we mean that the kaizen team will be working on a single process or even part of a single process within a single department, whether it be in the office or on the factory floor. Problems that are related to speed and waste are most appropriately tackled with Lean tools, which typically do not involve the same kind of in-depth data collection or statistical analysis that is more typical of the Six Sigma toolset.

Figure 9.1 shows a typical kaizen schedule compared to a typical DMAIC project schedule. As you can see, although kaizens use

Figure 9.1 Comparing DMAIC and kaizen projects

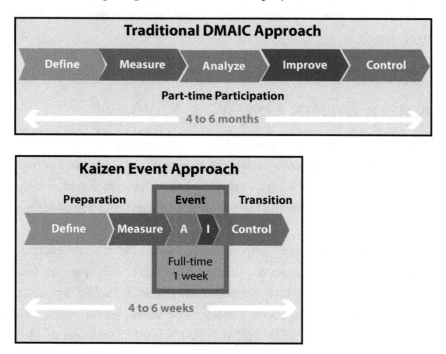

primarily Lean tools, they do so in the context of the Six Sigma DMAIC improvement phases.

Before the event week, the kaizen leader and other experts will usually do a draft value stream map (VSM) of the current-state process. At the start of the week, the full team finalizes this "as-is" map, then immediately begins to develop a future-state VSM, documenting the team's vision of how the process could operate in a way that would eliminate a specific problem and/or achieve a specific cycle-time target or quality goal. Team members spend the rest of the week identifying, testing, piloting, and implementing (as much as possible) the changes needed to achieve the future-state vision.

As noted, traditional kaizen events are very effective for solving smaller problems quickly. In fact, using a kaizen approach for any appropriately targeted and scaled projects in your pipeline can help you accelerate results compared to taking a traditional Lean Six Sigma project team model approach. But as we'll discuss next, this model of dedicating a week to improving a process can also be used on a larger scale.

ENTERPRISE KAIZENS

As the name implies, enterprise kaizens are used to tackle broad problems that span multiple parts of an organization. However, solving these problems is approached the same way as normal kaizen events: by using primarily Lean tools to identify and eliminate waste and achieve significant streamlining within a short timeline, including a one-week event.

However, because enterprise kaizens tackle broader issues, there are a number of differences between their structure and that of typical kaizen events. These differences are summarized in Table 9.1; we discuss most of them in this section.

Scope

The whole point of the enterprise kaizen approach is to tackle high-level processes, which by definition are going to stretch across multiple departments and possibly other divisions. Even so, you still have to avoid "scope creep" so that you don't end up trying to tackle the entire organization at once! One trick is to have the project leader keep a "parking lot" list of ideas that come up during the planning and execution of the kaizen week. That way, no good idea is lost, but at the same time, the team is able to stay focused on the main purpose of the week.

Team Size and Selection

The selection of team members is especially critical in an enterprise kaizen. Because the pool of candidates is quite large when you consider

TABLE 9.1 How enterprise kaizens differ

	Typical kaizen	Enterprise kaizen
Scope	Single process within one operation	Multiple processes crossing silos or department boundaries
Team size	7 or 8 is ideal; 10–15 is manageable	Depends on circumstances, but is often five to ten times as large (50+ people)
Team members	Usually obvious (the people working on the single process)	Requires more deliberate selection (involves a much larger pool of candidates)
Preparation requirements	Start a week or two before the event	Start at least a month before the event
Logistics	Single process within one operation; logistics fairly simple	Multiple processes crossing silos or department boundaries
Targeted level of VSM accuracy	At least 90 percent accurate for "as is"	Strive for a good skeleton (it would take far too long to achieve 90 percent accuracy on a process covering multiple departments)

all the people who interact with a process that crosses organizational boundaries, you need to be clear about the criteria you will use to pick those who will participate. Some key characteristics to consider are:

- *Expertise.* You want people who are experts in their part of the process.
- *Ability to think broadly.* Participants will need to think about what is best for the process as a whole, not just for their particular piece of it. You want people who can appreciate the larger picture of a bigger process.

- *Flexibility.* Participants will need to be able to examine issues from different perspectives and be interested in entertaining new ways of doing work. They need to be open to the ideas of other colleagues. You don't want people who come into the event thinking that they know what is "best."

- *Willingness to speak up.* One of the most important things that happen during a kaizen event is that people get to compare viewpoints and opinions. This is the crux of why you bring people together in the first place, and it is especially critical for an enterprise kaizen. If someone representing Step 1 of a big process is giving a presentation, you need the people representing the other steps to be willing to question the impact of that step on their own work. "What about XYZ, which we need for our step?" In almost every case, it will turn out that the individual making the presentation simply hadn't been aware of or thought about the downstream or upstream needs. This ability to get ideas from the whole process all at once is one of the reasons why you get so much leverage from an enterprise kaizen. Pick people who will have the confidence to contribute fully during the week.

Preparation

The basic schedule for an enterprise kaizen is the same as that for a regular kaizen: the event leaders will need to do some up-front preparation, followed by the week in which the full team comes together to do most of the work, followed by a period in which implementation issues are resolved and the changes are fully implemented. As noted in the previous section, this cycle can be as short as four to six weeks for regular kaizen events, but may be twice as long for enterprise kaizen projects.

For example, you will need time to conduct a number of briefings for the participants before the week begins. Remember, in a typical kaizen, people are working on a process that they know intimately. With an enterprise kaizen, the participants will need to understand a lot more about what happens before and after their pieces of the process. Also, if you have a large core or support process, the number of unknowns that the team needs to address could easily overwhelm the participants if they show up unprepared. There also isn't much time during the week to provide background information.

Making sure that the working groups will have all the support and resources that they need during the week is also important. For example, while the event leaders can make educated guesses ahead of time about data that the team may need, there are always unanticipated needs that arise. So there has to be someone available in each home office who can secure and transmit any requested data at a moment's notice (which gets quite challenging when global companies and multiple time zones are involved).

Logistics

Handling the logistics for a group of 50 to 80 people is exponentially more difficult than handling them for a group of less than 10! You need to plan all the transitions carefully, going from the initial large group kickoff to small group deliberations and conclusions, and then reconvening for the small group presentations. You will need enough trained kaizen facilitators so that each small group gets its own coach. You will also need to make arrangements—in terms of both staffing and materials—to make sure that you can capture all the ideas and update them as needed during both the small group and large group discussions.

The workflow of an enterprise kaizen is much the same as that for a regular kaizen, although you will need to have some time

FIGURE **9.2** Typical enterprise kaizen event schedule

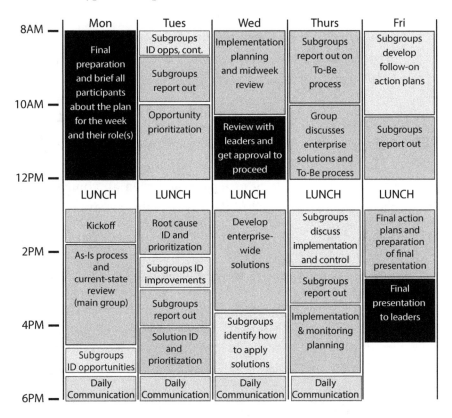

where all the participants are together, so that you can ensure alignment around goals, decisions, and commitments—as well as provide a venue where conflicts can be identified and resolved. But you need to allow time for smaller groups to get their work done. The way to handle this is through a mix of large group and small group work, as shown in Figure 9.2.

For example:

- After a full-group orientation at the beginning, divide the large group into smaller teams, each of which focuses on a small piece of the larger process.

- Each of the small work groups focus on a specific issue for a limited period of time (say, two hours).
- All groups reconvene, and one spokesperson for each group reports out.
- This pattern is repeated throughout the week.

In the first breakout session on Day 1, the small groups would discuss the shortfalls of the as-is performance of their part of the process, and talk about workarounds that are currently used to side-step problems. The working groups would then all come together, share their insights, and finalize the "as-is" value stream map.

Value Stream Mapping in an Enterprise kaizen

Creating value stream maps of the before and after process is a central part of almost every kaizen event, no matter what the scope. In an enterprise kaizen, however, you can't expect to go into as much detail as you would in a normal kaizen because of the time it would take to completely define the larger process that is under study. So the team will need to decide how much detail is sufficient to allow the session to be productive, but not so much detail that time is wasted in the minutiae.

Case Studies of Successful Enterprise kaizen Events

Now that you have a basic understanding of enterprise kaizen events, let's examine two cases. We'll start with a regional power company, whose experience illustrates many key features of enterprise kaizen,

and then revisit the hiring processes at the global company introduced at the beginning of the chapter.

Case 1: Joining the Modern Age

A regional power company was responsible for the distribution and
transmission of electricity across a large geographical area. It maintained all the high-tension wires and substations as well as the poles,
transformers, and wires going to businesses and residences. The
company had been around for decades and was known as a place
where employees would spend their entire careers. However, a large
proportion of the field workforce was nearing retirement.

For many years, this company had survived through guesswork
and experience. A large majority of the older workers had little
formal training, but had years of experience and knew their jobs
very well. There was little documentation or standardization of
processes; people were just used to doing whatever was needed to
get the job done. Their natural tendency was to develop individual
work-arounds for problems rather than to try to standardize a process. Their independence and "can do" attitude led to a very high
esprit de corps all around, which was often useful. For example, in
the face of weather that could cause power outages, employees did
not need to be told where to be and what to do; they already knew
the weaknesses of their system and would move into those areas
with little direction from headquarters.

However, the company had just gone through an extraordinary
increase in the demand for electricity because of expanding industries in the area, and expected more expansion in the near future. As a
result, they had just hired many younger, less experienced employees.

In the previous months, the power company had launched a few
individual improvement projects, but those were targeted at small
pieces of some key processes (such as monitoring the condition of
wooden utility poles). The leaders then realized that they needed an

approach that could tackle the much larger problem of the company's demographic doughnut hole—the loss of the accumulated experience of its near-retirement workforce and the need to quickly educate and train younger employees across all core processes in order to meet the increasing demand.

That's when the leaders decided to use the enterprise kaizen approach. They immediately launched an effort to develop two as-is value stream maps to document the two core processes; these initial VSMs were completed over a period of three weeks. It took a few more weeks to organize the logistics of identifying the right people that needed to participate in the enterprise kaizen and bring everyone together.

In what turned out to be the first of several enterprise kaizen events, the company decided to tackle one of its most important core processes: designing and building high-tension lines and substations for delivering electricity. The leaders ended up bringing together a group of 65 frontline workers and supervisors who worked on subprocesses such as production scheduling, switching, accounting, reporting, and so on. Every piece of this large design-build core process was represented.

As described earlier, the pattern of the week followed the usual kaizen model. The large group was divided into seven working teams, each of which finalized an as-is value stream map that had been started prior to the workshop. The working teams were then given the task of developing the future-state "to be" map for their piece of the process, identifying the necessary changes, and testing the new approaches as much as possible. Each day of the event followed a similar pattern: the working teams would meet for about 90 minutes, then all teams would come together and debrief each other on their progress. The whole-group sessions gave everyone a chance to ask questions and make suggestions, which helped keep the working teams aligned throughout the week.

The Importance of Senior Leadership Involvement

In what turned out to be a critical move, on the first day, a number of the company's senior leaders attended the session to talk about the importance of the work that was being conducted during the week. As we learned afterward, this simple step made a huge difference in two ways.

First, this company had a culture that was very resistant to change. People would try to "just hold tight" until changes had passed them by and everything went back to normal. That approach had worked in the past, in part because the senior leaders had never involved themselves in improvement efforts. With the senior leaders opening the meeting, the participants all knew that something was really different this time. They also knew that if they didn't produce during the week, the senior leaders would know it!

Second, because the participants had been briefed ahead of time, they knew that they were going to be asked to make major changes in the way work was done in their company. This made them extremely uncomfortable, since their work systems had not been changed in decades. But then they heard the senior leaders passing along the message, "We can't keep working the way we have been, or the company will be in danger of a takeover. We have to make changes." That convinced the participants that changes were both necessary and acceptable.

Throughout the week, the project leaders and advisors constantly made the rounds to ensure that each working team had what it needed to keep moving forward. They would ask questions like, "How are you doing? Do you have the right contacts to get the data you need? Do you have the right mix of people in your group to address the parts of the process that you've been assigned?" Senior leaders would ask these same questions of the project leaders during periodic debriefings throughout the week. This helped the participants realize that their managers were not just asking them to make changes, but also making sure that they had the resources they needed in order to do so.

By the end of the week, the kaizen team had a list of more than 110 action items. Each action item was reviewed during the final debriefing of the working teams to the group as a whole. At that time, the most knowledgeable person typically volunteered to take responsibility for an action item, so that each of the action items was assigned to an owner by the end of the week. Some action items had a proviso that they would be reviewed within a week to determine the fairness of the workload. The accountable person was required to determine a realistic completion date and plan the sequencing as it affected other action items.

The very last item of the week was a debriefing to senior management, during which the action items and accountabilities were once again reviewed, along with the accountable person's conclusions about timelines and resources. This senior management debriefing served two purposes. First, having people stand up in front of the group and say that they were accountable for providing a specific outcome by a specific date proved to be a powerful incentive for making sure that implementation would really occur in a timely fashion. Second, no one could claim afterward that he didn't understand what was expected of him, what the dependencies were, or what his role was, because it all happened in front of his peers and senior management. With the dependencies stated, everyone knew how shortcomings on his part would affect other improvement efforts.

Implementation and Outcomes

Implementation of the action items was accomplished in two phases: first in the northern part of the region, because that was where the demand for power was greatest, and then in the south. That way, the north got a quicker solution, because it needed to meet higher demand, and the south got a smoother implementation, since the people there had the opportunity to learn from the implementation in the north.

The list of action items included a mix of short-, medium-, and long-term actions. In the initial implementation in the north, the short- and medium-term actions were finished in two months. The longer-term actions required six to nine months, which was faster than normal for this company. As an example, the IT team involved in some of the most complicated actions had only positive feedback on the event. The team members said that normally it would have taken much longer than nine months, but the details that they were given as a result of the team's having created value stream maps made their job much easier.

Because people across the entire system agreed on how to do the work, handoffs between functions worked more smoothly than ever before, with much less need for rework. As part of the kaizen session, the team also reached a number of agreements on what decisions could be taken by subprocess and junior staff, and what had to be escalated to supervisors or upper managers. That led to quicker decision making on normal items and faster resolution even on issues that had to be escalated to senior leaders.

The overall result has been higher-quality decisions, made faster, with some assurance that all of the key factors had been considered. As a result of this effort, the subprocesses involved in the two main core operations work much faster than ever before. After six months, the cycle time was reduced by 22 percent for one core process and by

28 percent for a second process. In both cases, personnel felt that an additional 5 to 7 percent reduction was achievable.

Case 2: Revamping the Human Resources (HR) Processes

As we discussed earlier, the HR processes inside a large, fast-growing global company were unable to keep up with the demands for hiring technical specialists. After some initial discussions, we convinced them that the only way they could revamp the processes within six months to create a cycle time of less than two months was to use the enterprise kaizen approach.

There were four major pieces or silos in the HR process, and the two directors who owned the middle two silos were leading the project. They were extremely hard-working and adapted to the expanded scope quite readily. Each of them had originally anticipated creating a project team of four or five people, but when the scope was expanded, they knew that they needed to have a much larger team, one that represented all four silos in all regions of the world. They reviewed the related process flow charts and identified the team members who needed to be involved, then navigated the muddy waters of getting approvals.

Virtual Versus Physical Meetings

The project leaders briefly considered the option of using teleconferencing to conduct the enterprise kaizen event, but it is extremely difficult to get full participation in a virtual meeting. That's true even for small teams meeting for just an hour or two, let alone larger working groups meeting for the better part of a week across a set of global time zones. So they stuck with the plan to bring people together physically.

Once the approval for the kaizen event arrived, it took about seven weeks to get everything organized. During the actual kaizen week, the 55 invitees plus the kaizen coaches systematically went through the entire process spanning all four silos, similar to the process used by the power company described earlier. The improvements fell into four categories, which are summarized here along with notes on how much cycle time each one saved:

1. *Standardization.* This involved relatively easily implemented changes that cumulatively reduced cycle time by three work weeks. Examples include:
   - Design a common way to determine headcount needs across all geographies.
   - Standardize all HR databases and processes regarding job descriptions, job requisitions, and approval methods.
   - Drop non-value-added criminal checks in countries where laws prohibit them.
   - Design a global standard onboarding process.
2. *Eliminating redundant approvals and non-value-added activities.* This also involved relatively easy changes that reduced cycle time by an additional three work weeks.
   - No personnel requisition needed for jobs created due to a Plan Approval. (When a plan is approved as part of the strategy, the resources needed for that plan are also identified. This means that if personnel are in the approved plan, then an additional "personnel requisition" is not needed—that would mean approving the same thing twice.)
   - No approval needed once a replacement has been budgeted.
   - Limited approval needed for offers that fall within the preapproved salary range for the position.

- HR personnel do not schedule interviews; the hiring manager does.
- The hiring manager reviews the new hire's record for accuracy.

3. *Resequencing activities to create a more logical workflow and shorten the critical path.* This was a combination of easy and medium-difficulty changes that cut four work weeks from the cycle time.
   - HR is now involved at the start of the business planning process.
   - Agree on and execute the interview protocol within the local legal framework.
   - Be prepared to extend a verbal job offer on the day of the final interview.
   - Collect background authorization and forms during the final interview, as per local regulations.
   - When the requisition is approved, trigger the order for work tools based on position profile (laptop, mobile phone, office location, security and parking passes) so that everything is available on the employee's first day of work.
   - Ensure that finance and HR use common terms and operational definitions for headcount planning.
   - Arrange a seamless handoff of the headcount plan to accounting operations.

4. *Automation.* These were longer-term solutions, reducing the cycle time by another three work weeks.
   - Personnel planning, budgeting, and individual hiring approvals were made accessible to key executives globally, with e-mail notifications and updates in real time.
   - The hiring manager can now access the HR database with position descriptions, division or geographic

limitations, salary ranges, and government regulations checklists so that she can easily fill in the personnel requisition and trigger the approval process.

- Automatic updates of payroll, salary, and direct deposit information are provided to accounting operations upon hiring approval, to ensure timely and correct first payments to the new employees.

As a result of these changes, by the end of the enterprise kaizen event week, it looked as if it was possible to cut the cycle time by 42 percent, from 24 work weeks to just 14 work weeks. It took another 6 weeks after the event to get all of the short- and medium-term action items completed. Further work on the long-term (mostly automation) items took another 15 days (3 work weeks) out of the process, for an overall reduction in cycle time of 54 percent.

The overall result: it was now possible to complete the hiring process in half the time, quickly enough that job candidates were much less likely to be poached by competitors. Additionally, the HR personnel involved in the process, as well as the new hires, had a much more favorable opinion of the new process. While cost reduction wasn't a primary goal, the company saved more than $500,000 in printing costs by eliminating the need to print and mail HR materials to new hires.

Adding Enterprise kaizen to Your Toolbox

What we've found is that enterprise kaizens are very effective when a company has a major problem or improvement goal for a large process and not a lot of time to make it happen (as in Case 1 in this chapter). It is also the approach to take when several regular DMAIC projects are unable to make enough progress or get the commitment of team members without support from senior management to the improvement of a core process companywide (Case 2). Enterprise kaizens require more planning and dedication of resources than either traditional improvement projects or typical kaizen events, but that larger initial investment pays off in terms of how quickly you can implement a solution across the organization and generate significant results.

This approach is not limited to solving existing problems, but can be used under almost any circumstances to eliminate process waste across a system. For example, it is an effective way to streamline a process prior to the purchase or installation of new software such as SAP (and, as a by-product, reduce the need for expensive customization). It can also be used after a merger or acquisition as a way to bring together disparate groups to agree on a single system going forward, a system that can "borrow" the best from what each of the two systems had to offer. And the knowledgeable personnel involved can also create the integration plan for linking and integrating these new best solutions.

Consider the enterprise kaizen approach when you have a big problem to solve and not much time.

10

Linking Top to Bottom: Using Hoshin Planning for Strategy Deployment

WITH CHUCK COX

Years ago, an auto assembly plant was trying to "go green." In addition to using a variety of Lean Six Sigma methods to make improvements, they used a technique known as Hoshin Planning to communicate priorities throughout the entire plant. Was it successful? You be the judge.

We asked a forklift operator at this plant why he occasionally stopped at the assembly stations to check on whether empty cardboard boxes were protected from contamination (from waste paper, dirty cloth wipes, and the like). He said, "If we can reduce contamination, the plant makes more money from selling boxes for recycled cardboard than the value we get by using the cardboard as dunnage. That's how going green affects our bottom line." The forklift operator not only clearly understood his company's strategy, but also understood exactly what he could do to help the company implement that strategy and be successful.

Another company had a quite different challenge: during the economic downturn, growth and revenue had dropped dramatically, and the company needed to ramp up their new product development efforts in order to revive their aging product lines. But the leadership kept running into conflicts with competing demands for critical resources and equipment. It was only when they found a way to objectively evaluate resource requirements from all departments relative to strategic priorities that they were able to both keep daily operations working efficiently and develop a smooth product pipeline that could regularly deliver new products to market.

These stories perfectly illustrate the benefits of Hoshin Planning. When it is used correctly, people at *all* levels—not just senior executives—will be able to make a direct link between their objectives and the organization's business goals. Every employee will be able to make judgments every day about how to spend his time in ways that will contribute to strategic priorities. Deployment leaders will know what criteria to emphasize when selecting potential Lean Six Sigma projects, and business units will be able to work in concert to balance resource usage.

In this chapter, we will give a brief overview of the kinds of deployment problems that Hoshin Planning can help resolve, provide an overview of the methodology, and describe several types of applications.

DEPLOYMENT FAILURES THAT HOSHIN PLANNING CAN SOLVE

There are three common challenges associated with Lean Six Sigma deployments that may not seem connected at first glance, but that potentially have the same root cause.

The first—and one of the most common complaints heard about deployments—is a disconnect between Lean Six Sigma and business priorities, or the results that senior executives care about. This failure mode arises when "strategy development" and "project selection" operate independently of each other or when the links between them are unclear.

The second problem often occurs in companies that have pockets of success with their deployments. Eventually, they realize that what any successful department or process can achieve is limited by the quality and productivity of other business units. That is, poor performance in some other part of the organization puts a low ceiling on what the successful deployment areas can achieve.

The third problem is seen when different parts of an organization have very different operational needs. A classic example occurs in companies that have new product development activities whose timelines are either much longer or much shorter than the four-quarter annual planning cycle that other departments use. In these situations, balancing the use of resources is particularly tricky, and design projects can get shortchanged unless the organization can recognize conflicts and resolve them in a timely manner.

Do you see the common thread here? All of these problems are symptoms of poor connections between different parts of an organization. Or, looking at them another way, these problems can be resolved if the organization can make *better* connections between its moving parts: between strategic priorities and frontline projects; between functions along a value stream; or between teams that are competing for limited resources.

Making these kinds of connections is the purpose of Hoshin Planning. It helps organizations establish links between broad strategies, priorities for each division or department, and ultimately priorities for individual projects. Along the way, each piece of the puzzle gets to see how its priorities and goals contribute to the goals of every other piece, and how they all fit together to create strategic direction.

HOSHIN PLANNING BASICS

As you may know, Hoshin Planning goes by several other names, including the original Japanese term *Hoshin Kanri* and its English translation as "policy deployment." The latter label is perhaps the most accurate description: Hoshin Planning is a means for developing a strategy and related policies and also for ensuring that the strategy and policies are communicated clearly throughout the organization. What Hoshin Planning does that other planning methods seldom do is acknowledge that all elements of a business must be aligned and coordinated in order to achieve maximum performance. All the pieces of the puzzle have to be focused on shared goals and also be aware of what role each piece plays in achieving those goals.

The Hoshin Planning process begins like most traditional management methods, with people at the top level identifying business priorities that are cascaded downward to other areas of the organization. It follows the general pattern common to many planning strategies: a mission is translated into strategies, then into objectives, goals, and action items. But Hoshin Planning is very clear about which level of the organization is responsible for each component, as shown in Figure 10.1.

FIGURE **10.1** Hoshin planning cascade
The top level defines the organization's mission, strategies, and objectives (the left column). The middle layers of the organization turn the overall strategy into separate strategies, objectives, and goals for each division or department (center column). These departmental objectives are then turned into personal goals and action items for teams and individual employees (right column).

Though these basic elements of Hoshin Planning and traditional planning methods are similar, Hoshin Planning recognizes that true alignment cannot come from a downward-only cascading of goals imposed from the top—which has been the primary mode of communication used in the most popular planning techniques of the past half-century. Approaches like management by objectives (MBO), for example, do a good job of communicating information and priorities from the top levels of an organization down to the front lines, but that one-directional flow is where they stop.

To manage across boundaries and make connections between different moving parts, Hoshin Planning incorporates two important activities into the strategy development phase that are not included in other management planning approaches.

The first is that *discussions are focused on the value stream.* At the core of Hoshin Planning is an examination of how work gets done in the business, and especially how value is delivered to customers. Participants in the planning effort are asked to look for and share information about what is impeding the flow of work *into* and *out of* their work areas—in other words, where their connections to other functions and departments are not working well. (This horizontal perspective is a welcome component in organizations that have already begun to build a process-oriented mentality.)

These value stream discussions, along with the analysis of strategies and objectives, all happen through the second type of activity: a catchball process in which discussions among all of the affected parties allow issues and information to flow up, down, and across organizational divisions (Figure 10.2).

Through the catchball discussions, personnel at all levels of the hierarchy in both core and support functions are encouraged to ask questions of one another, and to take into account what they need if they are to operate efficiently and effectively, not just today but into the future. The discussions give each business area a chance to

FIGURE 10.2 Hoshin planning

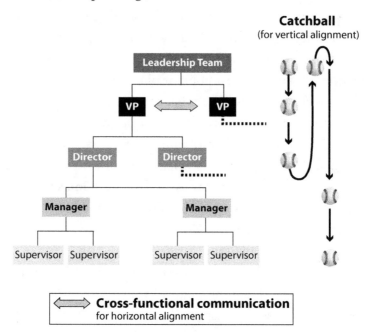

evaluate the demands it could face as a result of the strategy and objectives, compare those demands to its resources, and be clear about what it can and cannot commit to:

- Lower levels can evaluate and comment on feasibility and practicality before plans are finalized.
- Middle and upper levels can flag potential conflicts that need to be resolved.
- Upper levels will understand what policies and resources will be necessary so that goals can be reached.

As a result of this process, the organization can make sure that:

- High-level strategies reach into all the elements and areas of the organization and are translated into the language of that area's activities.

- All the moving parts of the organization are clear about the meaning and purpose of proposed goals.
- Each business has valid, win-win targets and goals established so that it doesn't have a negative impact on any other operation. These targets and goals will guide its daily activities and decision making throughout the upcoming year.

Honest Input Needed!

A challenge throughout the catchball discussions is to get honest, open communication and strive for true consensus, with all parties agreeing that the decisions that are made are best for the organization as a whole. It's not easy—which is one reason why organizations that adopt the Hoshin Planning method will need a designated facilitator. This individual will keep the discussions focused on the goals of each meeting and help groups navigate through tricky waters when differences of opinion arise.

An Iterative Process

Because the plans involve every part of the organization, it's not easy to implement Hoshin Planning from scratch and hit the mark in every instance—and this is especially true the first time through. Fortunately, unlike many traditional annual strategic plans, Hoshin Plans are meant to be living documents that are reviewed and revised regularly.

To make monitoring possible, part of the discussions includes asking and answering the question, "How will we measure whether we are meeting this goal?" For the most part, monitoring should be based on the systems that are already in place, including financial and budgeting activities. That means that the primary measures are typically financial performance metrics, but you also need to look for early detection measures—ways of monitoring operations that create warning signals of problems long before those problems become severe. These early warning signals are more likely to be the kinds of nonfinancial performance metrics discussed in Chapter 4.

Weave Monitoring into Ongoing Financial Processes

Ideally, the monitoring of the financial and nonfinancial measures is championed by the CFO or a rising star in the finance department who is excited about the implementation. The idea is to avoid having to build a new, parallel monitoring and measuring network when your finance department already has a system in place. It's much easier to add the monitoring of new metrics to an existing system than to start from scratch.

Although the finance department should be in charge of the system, numbers—whether hard or soft—are only part of the picture. Decisions should be based on a blend of data and judgment.

The cycle of planning, monitoring, and revising a Hoshin Plan is depicted in Figure 10.3.

Box 1 in Figure 10.3 shows that once a year, the business should evaluate and update its strategy and make sure that every part of the organization understands its role in making that strategy happen—this is the initial catchball phase of Hoshin Planning just discussed. Each business unit then needs to establish the performance measures it will use to track performance (box 2), and then continue the cycle to evaluate gaps, reevaluate priorities, and make adjustments as necessary (boxes 3, 4, and 5).

FIGURE **10.3** Hoshin planning in context

The reviews and adjustments should happen frequently (at least monthly), the first time through the process of creating and deploying the plan. In subsequent years, regular reviews, often quarterly or biannually, are done as a way to monitor implementation and ensure accountability.

Start Small

Because of the extra time commitment required—especially during the first pass at Hoshin Planning—many organizations will begin implementing Hoshin Planning in just one or two areas where the executives are most supportive. They then gradually expand the effort in subsequent years until the whole organization is involved. Admittedly, a Hoshin Planning process will require more time up front than some traditional planning methods, but the process gets easier and quicker with experience, and is typically much more valuable to the organization.

Documentation of the Alignment

There is a lot of talking involved in the catchball discussions, but talk is cheap. What matters is how well the organization can adhere to the agreements that are reached during the discussions. For that purpose, Hoshin Planning includes a number of tools that help document the commitments and goals in a way that illustrates the links between strategy and execution. One of the most important tools is an X matrix, which captures the commitments made by each group and also serves as a reminder of the links between strategies and actions. A schematic of an X matrix is shown in Figure 10.4.

The matrix has four main "wings" or components, each labeled in the center of the diagram. The example in Figure 10.4 depicts the format for an X matrix used at the top levels of an organization, so the four components in this version are:

- *Mission* (Area 1, the bottom wing)
- *Strategies* (Area 2, the left wing)
- *Objectives* (Area 3, the top wing)
- *Teams* (Area 4, the right wing)

The diagrams, like priorities, are cascaded down, with the focus of the wings being adjusted as needed to match the levels identified

FIGURE 10.4 Structure of an X matrix

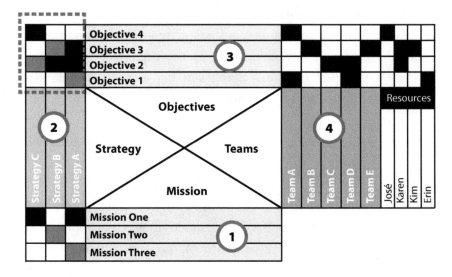

in Figure 10.1. The diagram for the level *below* the version in Figure 10.4, for example, would use Strategies, Objectives, Goals, and Individuals for the four wings.

X matrices look complicated because they summarize a lot of information, but in practice, the people who need to use them are the ones who build them over time, so the users will fully understand what decisions the matrix is capturing. The leaders working on their X matrix, for example, would fill in the wings in the ordered sequence (1 to 4) as decisions are made, then fill in the corners to indicate the relationships between two adjacent wings. For example, the shading of the cells in the highlighted upper left corner (boxed by the dotted line) shows the strength of the relationships between strategies and objectives (darker shading indicates stronger relationships). As shown in this example, Objective 4 is strongly connected to Strategy C, but it has no bearing on the other strategies.

There is a lot of information encapsulated in the matrix. Look at Team C, for example. You can see that it has responsibilities linked to Objective 2, which is connected to all three strategies. As a result, the team members' work contributes to all three missions.

As conditions change or conflicts arise—which they inevitably will—the leader at any given level of the organization can use an X matrix to figure out how changes at her level of command will affect those above and below her.

HOSHIN PLANNING IN ACTION

Hoshin Planning is a valuable method by itself, but it can be particularly helpful for Lean Six Sigma deployments, particularly those that are experiencing one or more of the deployment challenges described previously.

The first type of deployment challenge discussed earlier, for example, is the difficulty that many Lean Six Sigma deployments face in linking projects with business strategy. While that goal is intuitive, it can be difficult to implement because strategies may be defined only at a very high level or may not be well communicated.

Suppose a company has a strategy to decrease costs. In theory, that could mean that *any* cost-reduction project was aligned with that strategy. Hoshin Planning helps the organization do a much better job by forcing it to be significantly more specific. By the end of the planning process, the deployment team would know that the top priority for cost reduction would be a specific process within a designated business area. It would also know what key metrics will be used to measure success. With this type of information, the team members can select Lean Six Sigma projects with much greater confidence, knowing that the projects selected will actually make significant contributions to the cost-reduction strategy.

Here's another example related to the third deployment challenge introduced earlier: the difficulty in balancing resources and priorities between functions with very different business cycles. In these situations, tools like the X matrix can help the organization visualize the commitments of high-demand resources more easily and make decisions that will provide a steady stream of new offerings.

For example, consider a traditional manufacturing company that is nearing a hundred years old. For a decade spanning the late 1990s through the early 2000s, the company grew at a rate of 15 percent annually. Then, about six years ago, growth dropped precipitously, and revenue was off about 20 percent. Prior to this slowdown, there had been several cases of new product programs failing to meet deadlines for product launch and revenue targets, as well as several significant, unexpected delays in production operations.

Traditionally, this company had used a management by objectives planning approach, but the leaders realized that this method created problems in coordinating the deployment of its most expensive, rarest, and highest-impact resources. (For them, that meant system simulation, reliability, specialty polymer chemistry, and the use of expensive lab-testing assets.) The lack of critical resources had resulted in many interruptions and delays in operations, as well as delays in some critical high-value development projects.

To deal with these challenges, the company needed to more closely match resources to the activities necessary to carry out its strategies in both ongoing operations and new product development functions. And that's why the leaders turned to Hoshin Planning, using the methods outlined earlier in this chapter.

Initially, some participants in the Hoshin Planning exercise resented having to put in more time than they had invested during the previous planning cycles. But once the rollout and monitoring began, the universal sentiment changed in a positive direction. Managers realized that the structured monitoring system raised yellow flags that they could react to before there were significant issues. In addition:

- Project managers were pleased that there were fewer interruptions and delays on key projects because resources were available when needed—as agreed to among all affected areas in the plans. This level of predictability meant that more projects met the agreed-upon timelines, objectives, and results.

- Operations managers also acknowledged that the up-front work coupled with the monitoring systems greatly reduced delays and allowed them to deal with unexpected events more effectively.

Two years later, the senior leadership team asked the CFO to study the impact of implementing Hoshin Planning across the business. The CFO reported:

- Workload and revenue returned to roughly the same levels as before the downturn, but now it was possible to get all the work done and also maintain revenue with fewer staff members (a drop of 15 percent in full-time equivalents in operations and of 11 percent in projects).
- The company was able to bring new products and product enhancements to market much more quickly. Average delays on long projects (more than 12 months) dropped by two-thirds (from 6.1 months to 2.1 months); delays on short projects dropped by more than half (from 1.9 months to 0.7 month).
- Monitoring of the new metrics helped managers not only use their resources more effectively, but also identify problems that would have gone unnoticed before.
- The number of Lean Six Sigma projects per year almost doubled, and all of the new projects were clearly tied to corporate strategies.

This manufacturing company confirmed more than $15 million in Lean Six Sigma project savings over that time period. The overall conclusion was that using Hoshin Planning, which forced the up-front discussions about what resources would be necessary for a given goal or objective to be achieved, had enabled better planning and management at all levels.

VALUE OF HOSHIN PLANNING

Everyone knows that excellent strategic planning is difficult, but leading companies have a methodology and tools that can be applied across the organization to drive consensus on strategies, objectives, and goals. Hoshin Planning facilitates a successful path forward and provides a strong link between strategy and Lean Six Sigma.

Hoshin Planning is a strategic planning and deployment mechanism built around a multilevel view of the organization. The biggest value of the Hoshin Planning process arises from three points:

- The alignment that comes from the catchball phase, where a two-way dialogue up and down the organizational ladder and across functional boundaries helps the organization confirm and coordinate the implementation of strategic business priorities.
- The identification of metrics, tied to strategies, objectives, and teams, that are deployed across the business.
- The ability to revise and update plans because the means for monitoring progress and results have already been identified in the initial work.

Because of the multidimensional view of the organization that is developed, and its iterative nature, Hoshin Planning has a number of advantages over conventional planning and strategy development.

It gives leaders at all levels a more complete picture of the organization, which allows them to:

- Coordinate efforts that will improve the business as a whole, not just optimize individual departments or processes.
- Develop a *shared* understanding of resource priorities and allocations, which reduces internal conflict and allows for better up-front planning.
- Identify better metrics for running the business, which enables improved decision making.
- Make timely adjustments in response to changing business conditions.
- Seamlessly integrate strategy with the Lean Six Sigma deployment.

11

Solving Analysis Challenges with Specialized Tools

WITH LISA CUSTER AND JEFF KAHNE

When companies first get involved in Lean Six Sigma, the emphasis should be on using the data analysis tools that are most widely applicable and easiest to use. Almost every improvement project, for example, can benefit from using a basic process map to capture the work flow. Pareto charts and control charts are other tools that add value to most projects.

However, Lean Six Sigma also encompasses a wide range of more specialized data and process analysis tools. These tools are likely to be needed in fewer situations, but they provide insights and address complicated analysis issues that go beyond those that the basic tools can address. This chapter highlights four specialized tools that we believe deserve more attention.

Table 11.1 is a quick overview of the four tools we've chosen to highlight. In this chapter, we'll discuss the uses for each tool and present case studies showing how they have been used in real projects so

TABLE 11.1 Four specialized tools

Tool	Description	Unique Contribution	Uses
Shingo process map	A type of flowchart that combines the simple structure of a SIPOC (supplier–input–process–output–customer) chart with the data emphasis of a value stream map	One of the best ways to capture and understand the complexity and waste in a process and also identify front-to-back dependencies	Ideal when you have a large process or system and need a quick way to look end-to-end to identify improvement opportunities
Design of experiments	A structured approach to experimentation that allows the simultaneous testing of multiple factors	A data-based method for quantifying the relationships among factors that shape a product, process, or service	Discovery of the optimal *combination* of factors or settings for product or service design or process operations
Logistic regression	Like linear regression, logistic regression quantifies relationships between factors	Allows quantitative analysis for understanding causes or impacts even with response data that are not continuous measurements	Logistic regression is used to understand how different input factors affect an output. It can be used with binary, ordinal, or categorical responses
TRIZ	A structured solution-generation process for product and process design	Provides a mechanism for designers and engineers to push the boundaries of their creativity and resolve seemingly contradictory solution requirements	Use in any product or process design project where you are unsatisfied with your current options, want to expand the range of solutions, or want to resolve design challenges

that you can get a sense of the role they can play and how they can add value to your Lean Six Sigma deployment.

IDENTIFYING PROJECT OPPORTUNITIES USING SHINGO MAPS

Everyone who worked on the procure-to-pay operations for a global consumer products and pharmaceutical company felt that the process took too long and had too many errors. There was also a general sense that the company was spending more than was needed to comply with regulations that affected this part of the business.

The unhappiest people were those at the very end of the process because they often took the brunt of the blame when suppliers were not paid on time or paid the correct amount. Many of the problems they dealt with were the result of mistakes that had been made upstream. But where? And what changes would have the biggest impact on speed, efficiency, and improved compliance?

A SIPOC diagram or basic flowchart of this system would have had to be too simple to provide useful insights; a value stream map would provide useful data, but would not capture enough information about dependencies between steps. The tool that proved most useful here was a Shingo map, which combined the best characteristics of both of those tools: the simple process flow captured in a SIPOC diagram, supplemented by process data and analysis of the links between various steps.

To create the map, the company pulled together a team of process owners (one for each step). In this case, the process owners were VPs and directors because the process being studied was an end-to-end value stream. The team members spent a day and a half identifying the major steps and substeps in the process and identifying the dependencies between the steps. They filled the wall of a conference room with a large chart that captured all the SIPOC elements, including 8 major steps, which they further divided into about 20 substeps and 100 key activities (see Figure 11.1).

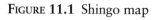

FIGURE 11.1 Shingo map

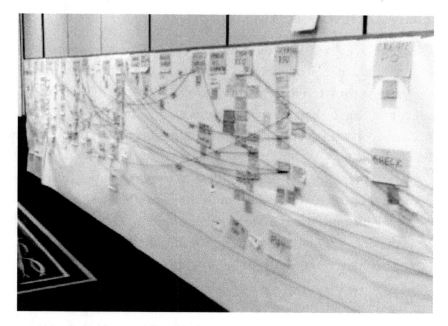

The lines across the chart are pieces of yarn that were used to identify rework—places downstream where work needed to be redone because of problems upstream. As you can see, there are a lot of lines, indicating that there were a lot of rework and dependencies in the process. (This won't be surprising to you if you've ever worked on a large administrative process like this.) As just one example, the end step, sending out a payment, could be delayed because someone had entered a wrong zip code back in the first step.

As a result of creating this chart, the team identified two major areas that needed improvement: (1) identifying the correct and approved source for a particular purchase, and (2) contracting with vendors. The team targeted 11 specific process steps that contributed the most waste and rework. Subsequent project teams were able to eliminate a total of 64 days of waiting and rework, with the potential for saving an additional 30 days through automation and parallel processing. Key improvements included standardizing orders and discounts, and identifying best practices concerning compliance. The company estimated that the improvements resulted in a 15 percent increase in efficiency, which translated into more than $100 million in cost savings.

Using Shingo Maps Successfully

- Shingo maps are not widely taught, but they are not hard for people who have prior process mapping or value stream mapping experience to master. Generally a Black Belt, Master Black Belt, or kaizen expert could teach himself how to create and use these charts or learn quickly by attending a course.
- Most important, *every major step in the process must be represented*. You don't need multiple representatives from different steps, but you need to include someone who knows what really happens "on the floor" in every area.

EXPLORING FACTOR RELATIONSHIPS WITH DESIGN OF EXPERIMENTS

Many people have been taught that the "scientific method" involves testing only one factor at a time so that the experimenter can isolate the impact of just that factor. In the real world, however, processes are affected by multiple factors at the same time, some of which have a big impact on the outcome, and some of which have very little impact. To make the picture more complex, some factors might interact with each other, meaning that the impact of one factor is affected by what's going on with another factor.

Design of experiments (DOE) is a tool that helps the team simultaneously evaluate the impact of multiple factors on a product, process, or service. The methodology can be used to:

- Quickly screen a large number of factors to identify which have the biggest impact on the outcome and which have little impact. This helps you zero in on the factors that will matter most.
- Identify the optimal combination of factor settings or conditions needed to meet a business need (provide the fastest service, produce the most reliable product, lower manufacturing costs, improve customer satisfaction, and so on).
- Identify meaningful interactions between factors.
- Develop a mathematical model to predict the output of interest.

Suppose, for example, that you wanted to identify what factors had the greatest impact on website effectiveness, as measured by the number of click-throughs (where visitors click to navigate to additional pages on the site). There are many, many factors to look at, such as the position of the banner, color schemes, balance of text and graphics, promotional links, and so on.

With one type of designed experiment, you can quickly screen a large number of factors to find out which are likely to have the biggest impact on results. With another type of designed experiment, you could then look at those factors and find out how to use them to achieve the maximum effect. This would also help you identify which of the factors, if any, had a significant influence on another factor, or an *interaction*. For example, maybe a visitor's reaction to the banner position is affected by the promotional links. A designed experiment will help quantify the impact of all the tested factors and identify interactions.

While designed experiments have historically been used most frequently in manufacturing situations (where a result can easily be measured numerically), they can also be used in transactional processes and for the design and development of new products and services. Here is one example of a designed experiment from the financial services industry.

DOE Case Study: Improve Credit Card Offer Return Rates

A major credit card company wanted to make sure that its marketing dollars were being put to good use by increasing the response rate from mailed advertisements. They wanted to determine what type of offer would lead to the highest rate of applications for it's card.

After some discussion, they settled on three factors that they wanted to test: introductory annual percentage rate (APR), duration of that APR, and whether information was printed on the outside of the envelope. They knew that the first two factors would have an impact, but they weren't sure how big that impact would be. They also weren't sure about the impact of the third factor. One line of thinking was to keep the envelope plain so that people would open it up out of curiosity; the other was that detailing the offer on the outside of the envelope would be better, so that people would know the good offer they were getting.

The type of designed experiment they chose required them to identify two controllable settings or levels for each factor; their decisions are captured in Table 11.2.

TABLE **11.2** Credit card DOE factors

Factors	Two Levels
Introductory APR	0% or 4%
Duration of APR	6 months or 9 months
Envelope type	Plain or detailing the offer

With three factors, each at two levels, there are eight possible combinations of factors to be tested, as shown in Figure 11.2. The company sent out 20,000 letters with each combination, for a total of 160,000 letters. The response they measured was the number of people from each combination who opened a new account.

FIGURE **11.2** Credit card experiment factors and levels

	APR	Duration	Envelope
Combination 1	0%	6 months	Plain
Combination 2	4%	6 months	Plain
Combination 3	0%	9 months	Plain
Combination 4	4%	9 months	Plain
Combination 5	0%	6 months	Detailed
Combination 6	4%	6 months	Detailed
Combination 7	0%	9 months	Detailed
Combination 8	4%	9 months	Detailed

All of the factors that they tested were significant (in the statistical sense). In this case, that was a good thing—sometimes the experimenters are hoping to discover what factors *aren't* important, but here it meant that the team had focused on the right factors. Some of the findings were obvious. People would rather have a lower introductory APR and have that APR last for a longer time period (the two combinations with shading). That's not unexpected; given an option, people will choose the best deal.

What they *didn't* expect, however, was the interaction between the introductory APR and the duration. It wasn't just that the response went up for the "lower APR/longer duration" combination compared to others—it went way up!

Also, it turned out that *14 percent more people* signed up for the credit card when it was sent in an envelope detailing the offer on the outside rather than a plain envelope. This is a very significant increase in response rate for a very minimal cost.

The best combination, therefore, was 7 (the row with the dark shading and white type). The marketing team was able to use this information to design future marketing programs, and this company now has some of the most popular and successful credit cards in the industry.

Using DOE Successfully

- Training on DOE is a standard component of many Black Belt and certainly all Master Black Belt training courses. So if you have BBs or MBBs in your organization, you probably already have the internal expertise needed to use this tool.
- To run a successful designed experiment, you have to be able to adjust and control the tested factors and measure the outcome numerically. For example, you would not use a designed experiment to study the impact of "outdoor temperature" or "incoming call volume" as input variables because you cannot control either of those factors. (As an aside,

continuous inputs that you do not control may be well analyzed with a regression analysis.)

● The requirement that factors be controllable with measurable responses is one reason why DOE is not as widely applicable as other tools. But when you do meet that criterion, you can develop a mathematical model to determine how to optimize your product, service, or process. And there are few other tools that are as powerful.

ANALYSIS TOOLS FOR DISCRETE DATA: LOGISTIC REGRESSION

Most of the statistics taught in basic improvement courses rely on what's known as *continuous data*, or measurements that can take on an infinite range of values. Measuring the length of time needed for a process step, for example, will generate continuous data—the time will usually fall within certain limits (say, one to two hours), but it can take on any value in between those limits.

However, sometimes the output of a process or action can take on only certain predefined values; this is referred to as *discrete or attribute data* in statistical circles. Sometimes these outcomes will be binary (yes/no, pass/fail), but they could also fall into categories (for example, red, green, or blue). Many of the basic statistical tools cannot be used on this kind of data—but there are other options that allow you to perform a quantitative analysis even if you don't have continuous data (see sidebar). One of these tools is called *logistic regression*.

Tests with Attribute Data

There are a number of choices of statistical tests for data that are not continuous.

- *Proportion tests* compare either a proportion to a standard or two proportions to each other—for example, the proportion of defects in a new invoicing process versus the proportion of defects in the old invoicing process.
- A *chi-squared test* is used in the scenario where there are multiple attribute input variables, and the response is also attribute data. For example, one could study the effect of using seat belts, texting, and drinking alcohol on traffic fatalities.
- *Logistic regression* is used when the input variable is continuous, but the response variable is attribute data. For example, to improve flight safety, NASA has studied the effect of temperature, a continuous measure, on the failure of O-ring seals, an attribute response.

If you've been through a Black Belt course or have been taught basic statistics, you probably know about linear regression: continuous data are gathered on two factors simultaneously and used to determine whether there is a correlation between the two factors. Logistic regression employs the same principle about looking for relationships, but the output data can be binary, ordinal, or categorical. Here's an example to illustrate how this tool can provide value in many situations.

The sales center of a financial services company had only a 37 percent close rate on incoming calls. They made a significant investment in training the workforce on a new sales process, hoping to see a big bump in sales afterward, but nothing happened. The close rate remained essentially the same.

The training vendor said that the lack of results was caused by people failing to follow their six-step method exactly. The trainers were particularly emphatic that if the workforce could at least get the first two steps right, then everything else would fall into place. Were they right? The company decided that the only way to tell was to use data.

Here's the setup: this company wanted to know whether the workforce was following the new six-step process and whether that affected sales. Measuring the outcome was easy; it was a simple yes/no—either a sale was made or it wasn't. But the challenge was how to measure whether people were following the six steps. That was an exercise in clarity and repeatability, as discussed in the sidebar.

Developing Clear Descriptions for "Fuzzy" Actions

You might think that it would be impossible to *measure* something as fuzzy as whether people conformed to a sales process, but it can be done as long as you put in some effort up front. This company worked with the training vendor to develop criteria associated with each of the steps (such as understanding "What does it take to do a good job on Step 1?").

They then had several experienced staff members listen to sample calls and try to evaluate whether those criteria were being met. Based on the results, the team tweaked the criteria and description and then did another round with a new team of expert "listeners." This cycle was repeated until the definitions of success were so clear that everyone evaluating a sample call would come to the same conclusion about whether the salesperson had performed that step correctly.

Once the criteria evaluation system was reliable, the company had a team listen to hundreds and hundreds of calls over a period of several weeks. At the end of the period, they had data on how many people performed each of the six sales steps correctly, and data on whether or not a call led to a sale. Figure 11.3 shows the percentage of time that the sales rep performed each of the steps correctly. As

FIGURE **11.3** Bar chart of the six steps

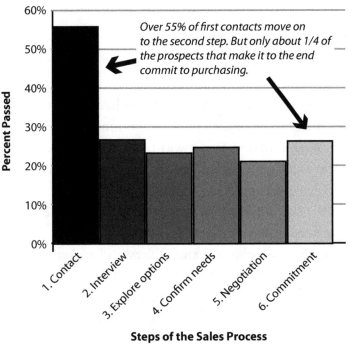

Steps of the Sales Process

you can see, a slight majority (nearly 56 percent) did well with Step 1, but less than 30 percent passed each of the other steps. If you add up these poor pass/fail rates, the reps did all six steps correctly only 6 percent of the time.

Some companies might have stopped at this point and decided to either abandon the new sales process or retrain everyone on the entire thing. But this company took the investigation one step further and performed a logistic regression analysis to see whether some steps were more important than others. The result is shown in Figure 11.4

FIGURE 11.4 Logistic regression table

Predictor	Coef	SE Coef	T	P
Constant	0.24969	0.06427	3.89	0.00
1. Contact	-0.08664	0.09845	-0.88	0.38
2. Interview	**0.2238**	**0.1141**	**1.96**	**0.05**
3. Explore options	-0.0969	0.1353	-0.72	0.47
4. Confirm needs	**0.2973**	**0.1545**	**1.92**	**0.05**
5. Negotiation	0.0612	0.1433	0.43	0.67
6. Commitment	0.0615	0.1233	0.50	0.61

Contrary to what the training vendor had told them—which was that the first and second steps were the most important—the company discovered that in fact it was the second and fourth steps that were most significant (meaning that they had the biggest impact on whether a sale was made). These were the steps that involved interviewing the customers to evaluate their needs (Step 2) and confirming those needs (Step 4). These two steps focused on communicating that the company had heard and understood what the customer was asking (as opposed to just taking an order). In other words, if the company listened and showed that they had heard the customer, they were exponentially more likely to convert than if they just talked about how good the company's products were.

With this more specific information in hand, the company could focus its resources on making sure that Steps 2 and 4 were done correctly. Instead of retraining everyone on the entire process, the company did a little remedial training on just those two key steps, and used ongoing coaching by managers to make sure that the workforce could do better at needs analysis and confirmation. Once the team implemented those improvements, the close rate started to rise and eventually approached the 60 percent goal that the company had set.

The key point we'd like you to take away from this case study is not about understanding the details of logistic regression. Rather, we just want you to be aware that there is a wide range of statistical tools that can be used to provide quantitative insights, even if you don't have continuous data or if there are problems with the original data set. In the case we covered here, logistic regression helped the company root out the causes of poor performance and focus on taking steps that would have the biggest impact on overall results.

Using Alternative Statistical Tools Successfully

- While most basic Black Belt programs focus on the more common statistical tools used with continuous, normal data, the tools for analyzing imperfect and noncontinuous data are usually covered only in advanced Master Black Belt training. If you have trained MBBs or statisticians in-house, turn to them for advice when you have situations where the more common tools do not apply.

- Fortunately, advances in software have simplified the data analysis for almost all of the less common statistical tools. Analyzing the data will not be the hard part! The challenge will come in knowing when to use the tools and making sure you can collect reliable data. Again, turn to your BBs, MBBs, or statisticians for help with those issues.

BEYOND BRAINSTORMING: RESOLVING DESIGN CONTRADICTIONS WITH TRIZ

It's hard to imagine a product design issue that does *not* involve a trade-off of some kind. You want a new product to be stronger, but also weigh less. Or to cost less, but still be durable. Or to withstand extreme temperatures, but remain pliable. In many situations, companies simply decide to make a hard choice to favor one factor or the other. But it doesn't have to be that way.

In the middle of the last century, a Russian scientist, Genrich Altshuller, made two remarkable observations after studying more than 200,000 patents. First, he realized that the level of inventiveness of a design was often linked to how well a design contradiction was solved. Second, he saw that the resolution of these design contradictions was the result of a fairly small number of inventive principles and strategies. That means that most of the trade-offs in product design that people were trying to resolve had already been resolved by someone else (or at least something very similar had already been done), even if it was for a different application.

The challenge the Russian scientist decided to attack was twofold:

- How to make the storehouse of existing knowledge concerning design trade-offs available to more people.
- How to answer the question, "What is the ideal final result?" As he realized, the goal in design should be to

find a solution that is optimal for all customers and stakeholders, not to find the best trade-offs per se. When the goal is an ideal result, it's easier to resist the temptation to take quick shortcuts that would suboptimize the design. It forces us to think more innovatively.

The result of this scientist's work is a product design methodology called TRIZ (most often pronounced like "trees"), which is a Russian acronym that roughly translates as the "theory of inventive problem solving." TRIZ is a methodology for resolving design contradictions. In contrast to brainstorming, which is essentially random idea generation, TRIZ takes an algorithmic approach: you have to first define your design challenge very specifically, identify the standard solutions for that contradiction, and then be creative in applying that idea to your own project. The five steps of TRIZ are listed in the sidebar and described here.

Five TRIZ Steps

The TRIZ solution approach is straightforward:

1. Identify current problems.
2. Translate to standard problems.
3. Look for a related, previously well-solved problem.
4. Investigate standard solutions.
5. Apply analogy-based thinking.

TRIZ Example

Because understanding design challenges can be difficult to explain if you're not well versed in the specific technical problem that is being solved, we'll use the example of trying to design a better soda can as a way to illustrate the TRIZ method. Here are the five steps and what they would mean for the redesign of a soda can.

1. *Identify current problems.* Identify the engineering system that is being studied, its primary function, and the ideal result.

   In the soda can example, the primary function of a soda can is to contain a beverage. The ideal desired result is to make the cans strong enough so that they can be stacked to human height without damage to the cans or the beverages inside.

2. *Translate to standard problems.* Restate the problem in terms of a physical or technical contradiction that could require a trade-off. This is often a challenging step because it takes some thought to see the links between a problem that you're trying to solve and the standard parameters identified in the TRIZ methodology.

   In the soda can example, there are two competing needs: (1) we want to lower our material costs, and (2) the can walls can be made thinner to reduce costs, but if we make the walls thinner, they cannot support as large a stacking load. So, the walls need to be thinner to lower material costs, but also thicker to support the weight of the stacked load.

3. *Look for a related, previously well-solved problem.* The original research identified 39 common engineering parameters and summarized how contradictions between them had previously been resolved. In this step, you use the problem statement developed in Step 2 to see which of the common engineering parameters apply to your situation.

   In the soda can example, we find the following information. (1) The list of standard parameters does not have a "thinner wall" parameter, but there is one called "length of fixed object" that can be applied here. (2) If we make the can wall thinner, the can will not support the stacking load. That relates to the parameter called "increase in stress."

4. *Investigate standard solutions.* The TRIZ methodology has a contradiction table that relates the standard engineering parameters to a list of inventive principles that Altshuller synthesized from his extensive patent research. Using this table will link the engineering challenges identified in Step 3 to design principles that could apply to your project.

   In the soda can example, the table points toward three solutions to the "length versus stress" contradiction: segmentation, spheroidality, and transformation.

5. *Apply analogy-based thinking.* Create as many unique and creative solutions as possible, based on the inventive principles.

   In the soda can example, there are three standard solutions that we could consider:

   a. *Segmentation.* Divide an object into independent parts. This could mean changes such as turning the typical smooth wall into a corrugated or wavy surface, which would increase the strength but allow the use of a thinner material.

   b. *Spheroidality.* Replace linear parts or flat surfaces with curved ones. The angle at which the lids are welded to the can could be changed to a curve.

   c. *Transformation of the physical and chemical states of an object.* Change an object's aggregate state, density distribution, degree of flexibility, or temperature. This would mean changing the material used for the can wall to a stronger metal alloy to increase the load-bearing capacity.

What we can't capture in an example in a book is that going through a TRIZ exercise is really fun. You bring people together and ask them to spend a half-day being creative. It's great for team building as well as problem solving. Usually, the results go well beyond the ideas represented in the reference tables; getting people into a creative mode often provides the inspiration for many additional options.

While TRIZ was originally developed for the design of new products, many of the principles apply to process design as well. Parameters such as speed, productivity, reliability, convenience, and complexity all still apply to most processes.

Using TRIZ Successfully

- Conducting a TRIZ analysis can often be done in a single afternoon, but it does require effort above and beyond traditional design work. That effort is worth it *if you want additional design concepts to consider.* If you're happy with the ideas your team is working with, then it may not be worth it to invest the time.
- TRIZ is not a widely taught tool. However, there are many online resources that someone from your organization could use to get up to speed relatively easily.
- Tracking down the links between your design challenges and previous solutions used to be a little tedious, but we have a free solution table on our website: www.firefly-consulting.com/triz/. You just need to input the design contradictions and it will provide the standard solutions.

THINKING OUT OF THE "BLACK BELT" BOX

Most people's impressions of Lean Six Sigma tools and methodologies come from what they or others learned during Black Belt training. The purpose of this chapter was to show that there are other process and data tools that go beyond the basics. We've covered four tools in this chapter, but there are many, many others. Leading deployments have taken steps beyond the standard Black Belt toolbox.

Our advice to you: if you encounter a situation in which the basic tools aren't appropriate or don't provide the level of analysis or insight that you need, your best reaction is to assume that there *is* a tool or method that can help—what you need to do is find it. Talk with MBBs, statisticians, or Lean Six Sigma experts inside or outside your company to determine what questions need to be answered and how to best answer them with data. Think outside the Black Belt box and you'll find a treasure trove of additional data tools that can solve your most challenging analysis needs.

12

Starting from Scratch

When and How to Use Product and Process Design Methodologies

WITH CHUCK COX

Most of us understand that innovation is enormously important. It's the only insurance against irrelevance. It's the only guarantee of long-term customer loyalty. It's the only strategy for outperforming a dismal economy.
—Gary Hamel

A company that manufactures medical equipment was facing a loss of market share in a line of advanced devices used for a particular type of specialized surgery. The company's leaders thought they could reverse the trend if they could conquer certain technological challenges that were common in this type of device. Doing so would require them to adapt technologies used in different kinds of applications and extend the functionality of old components—and to find a way to integrate both old and new into a high-performing, easily manufactured device. As if those challenges weren't enough, development of medical devices requires extraordinary care in design and manufacturing, since human welfare is on the line.

Here's another example: like many companies today, a printing business decided to expand into online offerings to remain competitive. However, the initial results were disappointing. The initiative failed to reach projected revenue targets while requiring far more resources than had been anticipated to keep the new offerings running smoothly. The company's leaders realized that they would need to evaluate their online services and potentially overhaul the way the process worked so that customers could have a seamless and positive printing experience no matter how they accessed the company's services.

The basic Lean and Six Sigma methods that people typically learn first are adaptable enough to fit a wide range of situations where the goal is to improve what already exists. But they are not as useful in situations like the ones that these two companies were facing. These were situations where the company had to design a new product or process from scratch, or to make radical changes in an existing product or process in order to achieve step-level gains in functionality or performance. To meet these challenges, you need a methodology that:

- Generates many more insights about customer needs and priorities.
- Emphasizes creativity and innovation so that you can go beyond what already exists inside your company or the marketplace.
- Explores multiple design alternatives so that you can be confident of getting the best possible solution.
- Helps create a smooth transition for implementation of the new product or service.

When to Use Design for Lean Six Sigma

Design for Lean Six Sigma is used whenever companies have a need to:

- Create more innovative products and services.
- Reduce time to market for new products and services.
- Develop higher-quality new or reinvented processes.
- Increase customer focus.
- Improve acceptance in the marketplace of new products or services.
- Improve product or service quality.
- Develop new processes that are efficient and effective.
- Improve the transition from design to manufacturing to commercialization.
- Reduce development and production costs.

The methodology we recommend to meet these needs is called Design for Lean Six Sigma (DfLSS). As with the basic Lean Six Sigma methodology, DfLSS combines the focus on speed and efficiency of Lean with the data-driven analysis of Six Sigma. But it includes a different suite of tools that allows for much more rigor in terms of:

- Gathering the voice of the customer (VOC)
- Finding creative solutions to meet customer requirements
- Developing design options that not only meet the functional requirements but are easy to produce, deliver, and support

DfLSS offers a structured approach that assists designers (whether product, service, or process) in moving from customer desires to design concepts and detailed designs, and finally to well-manufactured products or well-implemented services and processes. With DfLSS, design teams get the information they need in order to make good decisions early in the project, which leads to significant opportunities for cost reduction, quality improvement, and targeting of the true needs and wants of the customer.

DfLSS can generate big gains. For example, the medical device manufacturer regained its lost market share and then some! The online printing company generated several million dollars in additional revenue.

In this chapter, we'll talk about DfLSS and its core methodology. We will also show how the two companies introduced earlier used DfLSS to solve their process and product design challenges.

THE DESIGN METHODOLOGY

If you've worked with Six Sigma at all, you know that the core methodology is known as DMAIC, for Define–Measure–Analyze–Improve–Control. DfLSS has a similar core methodology known as DMEDI, for Define–Measure–Explore–Develop–Implement (Figure 12.1).

Though the first two steps of DMAIC and DMEDI sound the same—Define and Measure—in practice, they are quite different:

- *Define.* In a design situation, you aren't defining an existing problem (as you are with DMAIC); instead, you are defining the *opportunity*: what need exists that requires something brand new to be developed or something existing to be greatly overhauled?

FIGURE **12.1** The DMEDI Methodology

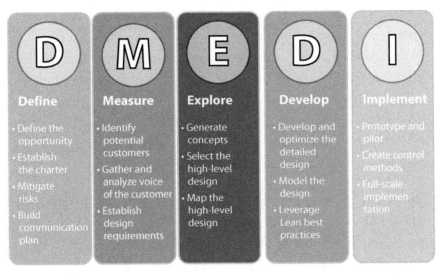

Define
- Define the opportunity
- Establish the charter
- Mitigate risks
- Build communication plan

Measure
- Identify potential customers
- Gather and analyze voice of the customer
- Establish design requirements

Explore
- Generate concepts
- Select the high-level design
- Map the high-level design

Develop
- Develop and optimize the detailed design
- Model the design
- Leverage Lean best practices

Implement
- Prototype and pilot
- Create control methods
- Full-scale implementation

- *Measure.* In the Measure phase of DMAIC, you gather data on an existing process or problem. But in a design project, nothing exists yet, so you are measuring the customer needs. To get a broad perspective, we use the term *customer* in the broadest possible sense, meaning anyone who will be involved with the new process, service, or product.

The rest of the steps involve the actual design work, including how the new or changed product or process will be launched. If you have not worked with the DfLSS methodology before, here is a quick overview, starting with the formation of the team.

Forming the Team

One aspect of the DfLSS approach that distinguishes it from typical design work is that key players with different perspectives are required to work together from the project's inception. Customer needs are not identified by marketing and then thrown over the wall to engineering; people working in an upstream part of a process are not allowed to ignore the needs of those working downstream. Instead, DfLSS projects rely on having cross-functional teams, on which every part of the product or process is represented. Because the different parts of the "design machinery" are communicating with one another from the start, there is far less rework than in typical design projects, and opportunities to innovate are more likely to come to the surface. As a result, DfLSS methods enable shorter development times, generating revenue or cost savings from the new product, service, or process more quickly.

Define: Understand and Document the Opportunity

As with any Lean Six Sigma project, the first steps are to define the desired outcome and establish a charter for the project (including goals and timeline) that has a clear tie to a specific element of the business strategy and a linkage to financial benefits. The team should also start to identify and mitigate risks, and establish the lines of communication among the team members, the sponsors, and other stakeholders.

The Define phase in DMEDI uses similar tools to the Define phase in DMAIC. However, it can be more challenging because the opportunity is less clearly defined. Getting stakeholder alignment from the start is absolutely critical.

Define Overview

Steps
Define the opportunity
Establish the charter
Plan the project
Mitigate risk
Build a communication plan

Tools/Deliverables
  Business case
  Project charter
  Project plan
  Risk management plan
  Communication plan

Measure: Gather the VOC and Translate into Prioritized Requirements for Design

The Measure phase is where a design project begins to look very different from a normal improvement project because the focus of the measurement is not on problems, but on customer needs. The team is required to establish what the customer mandate is: What are the needs that are not being met completely by the current processes or products?

This goal is sometimes referred to as gathering the "heart of the customer," which means understanding the customers' true needs and bringing an offering to market (or to the internal organization) that has compelling value.

A wide range of tools and methods are used to achieve this goal. Often teams will start with customer experience mapping, which we introduced in Chapter 7. Customer experience maps help ensure that all the touch points with the customer are evaluated. In this approach, you consider not just the core product, but how it is selected, purchased, delivered, installed, supported, and replaced—its entire life cycle with your customer—and look for new insights. This gives the team the opportunity to differentiate the product or process at every point where there is contact with customers.

The team gathers information on customer needs from many sources—interviews, surveys, focus groups, and so on—and organizes the information, looking for themes. The team can then use tools such as quality function deployment (QFD, introduced in Chapter 7), the Kano model, and conjoint analysis studies for additional analysis. These tools will help the team members understand those needs more deeply and translate them into requirements for the design. Additionally, they will define potential trade-offs on features and price based on how customers prioritize their needs. The role of QFD, for example, is discussed in the sidebar on the next page.

Understanding Customer Needs with the Kano Model

The Kano model is a framework for the classification of customer needs into basic needs, satisfiers, and delighters. Basic needs are the minimum requirements to get into the marketplace. In an automobile, brakes would be a basic need. In the hotel business, towels and beds would be an example of minimum requirements. Satisfiers, or performance needs, increase satisfaction by the degree to which they are implemented. For example, good gas mileage is a performance need: the better the gas mileage, the better the customer likes it. In hotels, features like cable television, a coffeemaker in your room, and frequent guest points are all satisfiers. Delighters are the things that go above and beyond. The customer doesn't expect them, but is delighted by them. In an automobile, navigation systems and satellite radio have been recent delighters. Hotels try to delight their customers with premium benefits that they did not expect, such as spa-style showers and advanced fitness equipment. Notice that over time, the delighters become satisfiers, and eventually basic needs. High-speed Internet was a real delighter at a hotel when it was first introduced. It is now an expected requirement. The Kano model can be incorporated in interviews or surveys to ensure that we get a complete view of all types of requirements. It also helps us understand the evolution of requirements over time and plan for future product line enhancements.

QFD at the Core of DfLSS

As noted in Chapter 7, QFD is one of the key tools used in design work, and therefore one of the most important tools in DfLSS. QFD is used to translate the customer needs into measurable, prioritized, critical customer requirements that the team can use in design. It brings together customer data, market data, and internal capability data—all in one diagram. A good QFD will also include benchmarking information, correlations where trade-offs may be needed, and established targets.

The first section of a QFD diagram documents the voice of the customer. There are other sections that translate these needs into design information, documenting answers to questions such as:

- How well do we and our competitors currently meet these requirements (competitive comparison)?

- Where should we focus our efforts for maximum return (competitive comparison, priority)?
- What can we measure or control to ensure that the customer requirements are met (critical customer requirements)?
- How do our proposed design requirements relate to our customer needs (interrelationship matrix)?
- What design trade-offs need to be analyzed (correlation matrix)?

While implementing QFD may sound time-consuming, it shortens the overall design time because it keeps teams focused on what matters to customers. In that way, QFD helps the team get it right the first time, and thus avoid months of disagreements and rework down the road. QFD fosters the rich discussion needed among the owners of all of the design elements early in the process, when the elements are still fluid and can easily (and inexpensively) be changed. This also helps the team bring potential risks to the surface and deal with them early on.

The most time-consuming part of the QFD process isn't executing the QFD, it is gathering and analyzing the voice of the customer, an activity I'm sure we all would agree is very important!

Conducting the Measure phase well is one of the most critical aspects of DfLSS. Everything else about the product or process design cascades down from what is learned about customer needs and priorities. The metrics and targets that result from this work should be clearly communicated to all participants. They make project management easier; for example, data can more clearly illustrate shortfalls or gaps in science or engineering. Having good data allows teams to identify potential risks much earlier in the design cycle, which allows them to reduce or mitigate those risks, or eliminate them altogether.

Measure Overview

Steps
> Identify potential customers
> Gather and analyze the voice of the customer (VOC)
> Identify product, service, or process design requirements

Tools/Deliverables
> Customer experience mapping
> Market segmentation
> Kano model
> VOC plan
> Interviews
> Surveys
> Affinity diagram, a tool for organizing and synthesizing
> customer information. If the voice of the customer
> data are complex, KJ analysis, a more advanced and
> structured approach, is recommended.
> Structure tree
> QFD
> Scorecard

Explore: Explore Alternatives for High-Level Design

The third phase of DMEDI, Explore, is where you draw on the creativity of the design team to come up with new concepts for meeting customer needs. And that's the secret to success—you want to bring in new ideas, not simply rely on what has been done before.

To do this well, teams should experiment with multiple design solutions and test them with customers. Teams can take advantage of alternative idea generation techniques, requirements and functional analysis, and TRIZ (the Russian acronym for theory of inventive problem solving) to generate multiple concepts that are original and unique. Customer dialogue and feedback are integral to the process to ensure acceptance in the marketplace. (For more information on TRIZ, see Chapter 11.)

One of the purposes of the Explore step is to challenge the orthodoxies in your industry—the way things have historically been done. By challenging the orthodoxies, a team can overcome false limitations on the feasible design space. Once an orthodoxy has been identified, you'll wonder why new solutions weren't developed earlier.

Consider this example: Nestlé was the first company to introduce ready-to-bake cookies, even though its competitor Pillsbury had been selling refrigerated cookie dough in a tube for years. Theoretically, Pillsbury should have been in the best position to bring the next round of innovations to market. But Nestlé challenged the convention that "easy-bake cookies must come in a tube" and brought to market a new product that offered customers additional convenience. It was the first company to offer prescored refrigerated cookie dough—no slicing needed—so the cookies could go directly from the package to the baking sheet. Nestlé has continued to expand the line with prescored holiday cookies, as well as "Nestlé's Toll House Ultimates," a prescored line of cookies that features higher-quality ingredients. Through this innovation, Nestlé stole significant market share from Pillsbury and created one of the highest-margin products in the category.

What are the orthodoxies that you could challenge in your industry?

Explore Overview

Steps
Generate concepts
Select the high-level design
Map the high-level design

Tools/Deliverables
Functional analysis
Idea generation techniques
TRIZ
Concept generation
Pugh concept selection, an approach for selecting
the best solution from multiple options, based on
predefined and agreed-upon criteria
Analytic hierarchy process, a tool for comparing and
prioritizing customer needs

Develop: Develop and Optimize the Detailed Design

The purpose of DfLSS is to bring to market products and services
that the customer will value and pay for, or to develop new processes
that will help a business operate more efficiently and effectively. The
work of translating the creative ideas into a useful, practical solution
starts here in the Develop phase.

Design teams have a variety of options to assist them in developing a product that is easy to produce and deliver, including:

- Simulating or modeling the new process or product
- Using mistake-proofing concepts to make a product that is
  impossible to misuse or mismanufacture

- Replicating portions of design concepts to minimize product complexity across the product portfolio
- Minimizing the complexity of a product's bill of materials
- Using customization techniques to lock in design options late in the process
- Using target costing, a method for aligning product costs with the functions that provide the most value to the customer

Similar "ease of design/use" concepts apply in process and service situations as well. In process design, the team members define the new process at a more detailed level in this phase. They also identify interfaces with downstream, upstream, and adjacent processes. This helps in several ways:

- Determining how to leverage these linkages (for example, a minor change in an upstream process might make the new process more efficient)
- Anticipating the ripple effects (positive or negative) of changes made in any part of the process (and helping the organization avoid any inadvertent negative impacts of changes)

Develop Overview

Steps

Develop and optimize the detailed design.

Model the design.

Analyze new process/product risk.

Leverage Lean best practices.

Tools/Deliverables
  Input-output mapping
  Detailed process mapping
  DFMEA (design failure modes and effects analysis)
  Discrete event simulation (Monte Carlo)
  Design of experiments (DOE)
  Conjoint studies
  Target costing
  Design for manufacture and assembly

Implement: Validate the Design and Implement It

In the Implement phase, the product or service is piloted, a control plan is developed, and the new product or service is launched—the sidebar on the next page. Pilot testing techniques are intended to bring risks to the surface and characterize them, as well as to demonstrate that the goals cited in a design project's charter have been met. For a product, piloting can mean building a functioning prototype that is shown (or given) to selected users. For a process, piloting can mean creating a simulation model that shows the process's behavior under selected stresses, or rolling out the new process in a limited area.

All of the tools from the Control phase of DMAIC are applicable here. We want the launch of the product, or the implementation of the new process, to go as smoothly as possible, and we want the performance to be sustained at or above its targeted level in the long term.

Implement Overview

Steps
> Prototype and pilot
> Create control methods
> Full-scale implementation

Tools/Deliverables
> Pilot
> Process control plan
> Visual process controls
> Control charts
> Implementation plan

DFLSS CASE STUDIES

Now that you have an understanding of the basic methodology, let's revisit the two case studies introduced at the beginning of this chapter.

Case 1: Product Innovation

As you may recall from the beginning of this chapter, a medical equipment manufacturer was eager to take advantage of a market opportunity by developing an advanced device used for a specialized type of surgery. Previously, the company had tried to rush a product to market, but it had turned into a major failure. Also, many prior design projects had been slow, and were fraught with an endless stream of minor issues and subsequent delays.

The initial analysis revealed that the new product would include 17 interconnected modules, of which 6 were brand new to this

particular application (the technologies had been used in components for other industries, but not in this particular kind of machine,
which demanded high reliability) and several others would need
substantial changes. The need to conquer a number of technological problems in one design effort, and with a severely constrained
time frame, were two reasons that the company embraced the DfLSS
methodology.

Another reason for turning to DfLSS was that the company
knew from experience that the cycle from the idea to a successful launch has a lot of moving parts that need to be coordinated.
There are many opportunities for even well-managed projects to go
off track. The challenges in this case were typical of those found in
many design projects. Here are five common risks encountered by
development projects, and how this company avoided them through
its use of DfLSS:

1. *Failure to understand the customer needs.* One reason that
    this company's previous product had gone astray was that
    it had relied solely on its engineers to come up with design
    ideas. The DfLSS methodology encourages teams to think
    as broadly as possible about sources of information—
    including various customer groups along the entire value
    chain—that can be tapped repeatedly throughout the design
    process.

    Application. This company ended up developing a
    customer group consisting of 40 doctors from around the
    globe and a technical advisory council of sophisticated users
    that they could convene as needed. This allowed them to
    get feedback on ideas, hypotheses, and design suggestions
    very quickly at multiple points in the project.

2. *Lack of governance over how decisions are made.*
    Unfortunately, a common problem we've observed in design

projects is the tendency to make decisions on the basis of power, authority, influence, or untested assumptions, instead of on data about customer needs and proven capabilities of the technology. DfLSS is rooted in data-based decision making. It also encourages design teams and their managers to agree up front about how decisions will be made and which players will have what level of authority. The training and experience of the Green Belt and Black Belt project leaders, and the structure of the DfLSS tools, encourage the most knowledgeable people to be involved in the various tasks. The structure results in a "thread of information," with the outputs of the tools used early in the process serving as inputs to the tools used later in the sequence. Decisions are made based on the data and the resulting information, with prompting from the road map.

Application. In this case, the company knew that when surgeons are performing complex surgeries, they often have to be able to control multiple aspects of the equipment at the same time. Their hands are working on high-priority, high-precision tasks, and their feet are controlling other devices. Using a foot control was not new, but based on the VOC, the surgeons wanted a nonlinear output with a "sweet spot" in the middle of its travel. The design concepts were initially difficult for the engineers to agree on. Then, a component subproject leader used the Analytical Hierarchy Process and the Pugh concept selection matrix to evaluate the performance of alternative designs with a small group of surgeons. The group of experts decided what configuration best met their needs. The output from this exercise was the input to the firmware of the foot controller manufacturer.

3. *Costly miscommunication (or noncommunication) among all the players.* Another problem we see in design projects is dysfunctional communication among the

marketing team, the design team, engineers, suppliers
or vendors, manufacturing, and/or people involved in
providing customer support. The structure of the DMEDI
methodology is such that teams cannot proceed without
talking directly to customers, both internal and external.
With this feedback, they can then clearly define up front
which customer needs constitute the value proposition,
and how much more valuable one need is compared to
the others. That means that there is a consistent source
of definitive information that all players can refer to, and
against which the results of all activities will be checked.
There is also an expectation of ongoing communication
within the cross-functional team.

Application. For this product, the foot control proved
to be a difficult component to source given the desired
performance. The initial conclusion that there should be
one "sweet spot" proved to be erroneous—once the chosen
design was communicated to likely users, it quickly became
evident that there was not one preferred configuration,
but several. Fortunately, the chosen design was flexible, so
when the prototype was being tested with a larger group,
it was possible to identify four different configurations that
fulfilled the spectrum of user performance expectations.
The ability to communicate different alternatives quickly
and accurately allowed a significantly better design to be
developed. The designers felt much better about their final
design—as did the foot control manufacturer. They said
that they had never worked so closely with an end user and
that they felt well guided in their design efforts at every
step. With the DfLSS approach and tools, they never wasted
time and effort.

4. *Nonalignment within the design team, or between the
   team and its managers, about goals and targets.* One of

the primary purposes of the QFD tool used in DfLSS is to document what customers say about their requirements and how that links to technical metrics and targets. Having those targets documented early on provides a useful guidepost for reference throughout the rest of the project. The designers and managers can challenge one another: Is what we're doing going to help us achieve our targets?

Application. The medical device being developed, for example, included a motor that needed to meet a specific rpm target. At times during the project, the team leader would say to the engineers, "If what you're doing will not help us achieve the rpm target, it may be useful at some point, but not on this project." That helped keep the engineers focused on work that was of value to the immediate issue.

5. *Delays that cause the product to be late to market.* Most companies we've worked with have an optimal time for releasing new products, often related to industry events or seasonal patterns. If they lose a month or two in the development process, they miss the window and may as well move on to the next product cycle. DfLSS projects produce results much faster than typical design projects because they avoid the sources of delays.

   Application. New developments in medicine are often released at major focused conferences. In the case of the surgical machine, the major international conference was held every two years. In the past, designing a new machine had taken 24 months. The challenge for this company was that the senior leaders hadn't realized how profound the shortfall in the previous design was until there were only 18 months until the next conference. To reverse the market share decline, they needed a much better product, with a design that addressed several old issues, but that added innovation in other areas. They needed a working prototype for the conference in less than 19 months—which the DfLSS approach delivered!

In part because the company was able to avoid and manage these risks much better than at any time in the past, this project—one of the most challenging it had ever tackled—was completed within 18 months compared to the usual timeline of 2 years. With the release of the new device, the decline in market share stopped, and in 6 months, it was up 9 percent!

Good, Fast, *and* Cheap

There's an old saying among engineers that you can have only products that meet two of the three basic criteria—good, fast, and cheap—not all three. That's not true with DfLSS! It allows the team members to develop high-quality products more quickly than is usually believed possible, while making them cost-effective based on the customer's value perspective (initial cost, support cost, or life-cycle cost).

Case 2: Process Innovation – Developing an Online Printing Process

The charter for the team assigned to redesign the online print experience for customers also included the need to develop new processes for resolving customer problems. To fully understand the needs and demands placed on the process, the team contacted representatives from five stakeholder groups. During the Measure phase, the team members asked each group questions so that they could understand that group's needs and interests. Table 12.1 gives a high-level summary of the much more detailed information about the interests of each group.

TABLE 12.1 Summary of stakeholder interests

Group	Interests
Customers	● High-quality product delivered on time ● Access to consistent support regardless of the channel (web, phone, or retail center) ● Strong support after the order is placed (including visibility into order status)
Corporate print services	● Want to ensure that the company can deliver an exceptional customer experience because competition in the market is tough ● Concerned about their role in the new process, including the potential need to handle delivery of orders placed online
Third-party vendor that does the printing	● Wants the process to be as seamless as possible ● Has no interest in dealing directly with customers
Corporate IT/web development group	● Focused on IT integration ● Wants to reuse existing and known technologies as much as possible
Corporate marketing	● Wants to drive new sales through this venture

One of the main insights from this phase was the high level of confusion about roles and responsibilities because of a third party being involved, along with multiple internal customer groups. Metrics and targets were also unclear.

In subsequent QFD analysis, the team did some benchmarking to establish performance goals. The competitive benchmarking, in particular, proved to be eye-opening: While the company thought it had performance comparable to that of other online printing services, the team members realized that customers were actually comparing their online printing experience not just with other printers, but also with other online shopping experiences (such as Walmart.com or Amazon.com). This helped the team members understand that to meet customer needs, they would need to improve the customer's experience by providing greater visibility into order status, as well as creating an easy cross-channel refund process and, additionally, improving postsales support.

During the Measure phase, the team saw immediately that there were limited existing data on the current online print service performance, except for the overall revenue. Because of the need to juggle demands from multiple stakeholders and to maintain clarity concerning roles and responsibilities, the team established a scorecard of critical metrics in three categories:

1. *Customer experience.* While the business was focused on the revenue growth opportunity, customers would need to have a great experience if the endeavor was to be successful in the long term. Metrics were implemented to gather data about the ease of use of the website, new customer acquisitions, reorder rates, and customer complaints.

2. *Financial metrics.* This included both revenue and profitability metrics.

3. *Internal processes.* The level of internal support required for the new venture was much higher than had been anticipated. Data were captured on the number of support resources needed to improve the customer experience.

Armed with a significant amount of feedback from both internal and external customers, and a new plan to measure performance, the team was able to design a new process that would provide the customer with a seamless experience, sales support throughout the process, and timely and efficient issue resolution. While there were many improvements implemented as part of the new design, the biggest area of impact was in the up-front process where the customer initiated the project and created the order. Revising this up-front work enabled better service delivery and prevented errors downstream in the process.

The DfLSS approach provided the print services design team with a structure and tools that allowed it to move through the development in a systematic manner, addressing the concerns of a complicated group of stakeholders. After just a five-month project, the service was back on target, delivering profitable growth.

Bonus Process Design Case Study

A large-equipment manufacturer often incorporated custom features or capabilities to suit customer needs. That required the manufacturer to involve teams of specialty engineers throughout the design and production phases. However, these engineering specialists were scattered around the globe, which added enormous amounts of complexity and time to many projects. The original organizational structure was expensive to staff, and it didn't have a particularly good relationship with the internal organization that was responsible for the overall equipment. In addition, customers were not particularly impressed with the resulting designs.

To address these problems, the company launched a DfLSS project to see how they could redesign the specialty engineering process. The team members met with a wide range of internal and end user customers to identify process requirements. This was the first time that the specialty engineering organization had actively solicited feedback from their partners in the downstream process!

Once the team members had the requirements, they used a Pugh matrix to evaluate the feasibility of 20 different models that they had developed for the new engineering function. Ultimately, they settled on the option of developing a centralized Center of Excellence for Engineering. The company discovered that this approach not only allowed a more coordinated response from engineering to customer requests, but also led to far greater innovation, because the best engineering minds were able to collaborate more easily.

The project took only a few months. In addition to improving the quality of the specialized designs, which was the primary objective, the project also ended up saving the company $1.5 million annually. The company continued the practice of gathering ongoing feedback, and customers reported that the new center provided them with higher-quality, more innovative designs for meeting their requirements.

Deploying DfLSS

The proportion of Lean Six Sigma projects that will involve design work varies greatly from business to business. In some, it may be as low as 10 to 20 percent of the project portfolio; in others, it could easily reach 50 percent or more. Projects involving design often require a larger up-front investment of time and resources, but provide a much greater return than typical Lean Six Sigma improvement projects. To make the investment in DfLSS worthwhile, you should:

- *Ensure executive alignment.* As in Lean Six Sigma, executive alignment is critical for success with DfLSS; the value of this commitment cannot be overstated. Conducting a readiness assessment can identify potential deployment allies, as well as uncover any problems that will need to be resolved if the deployment is to be successful. Projects that are crucial to the new product development strategy or projects that will enable a step-function improvement in an internal process are the ones that will generate the most enthusiasm within the business. They will catch the interest of the leadership team, thus helping to gain buy-in.

- *Host a dedicated launch event to introduce the effort.* Prior to beginning training or project work, it is important to get everyone on the same page. Launch events are valuable because they engage the leadership, educate key personnel, increase awareness, and build energy and alignment for the program. Additionally, they signal to the rest of the organization that changes are coming and that these changes have the senior leadership's endorsement.

- *Integrate product DfLSS with the existing new product development process.* Most companies have an existing new product development process. Thinking ahead to how the DfLSS tools and road map will integrate with any existing approach minimizes confusion and provides opportunities to streamline the overall process. If the business does not already have a procedure for developing new products, the DfLSS road map provides a good starting point.

- *Integrate process DfLSS with the existing Lean Six Sigma deployment.* Some companies launch DfLSS work as an independent stream of activities focused on product and service design or redesign. However, there is a lot of overlap between DfLSS work and typical LSS projects in terms of the basic improvement and team management skills needed—meaning that the two types of projects may compete for the same resources. In addition, history has shown that anywhere from 10 to 20 percent of projects often end up requiring DfLSS methods to achieve the level of improvement required. If your company has both LSS and DfLSS types of project work, look for ways to integrate the two efforts. For example, will your deployment team have the skills to lead design work as well as improvement work, or will you need to add new expertise to the team?

- *Offer hands-on training opportunities.* DfLSS training can be conducted in a traditional LSS multiweek format, but the greatest benefit often results from immediate application of the tools on high-priority projects. For small deployments, another option is using a blended training/coaching model, where part of the day is devoted to training, followed by just-in-time project work where participants have immediate access to the MBBs who are doing the training. This has the benefit of not only educating the project leaders about the DfLSS tools, but also reinforcing that learning with immediate application. Many organizations decide to train all members of the design team together. With this approach, the entire team understands the tools and can use the classroom exercise time to make real progress on their project.

USING DfLSS FOR COMPETITIVE ADVANTAGE

Leading deployments are able to tackle new design challenges and create innovative, customer-focused solutions. There is no other methodology that allows you to move as fast as DfLSS, nor that allows you to capitalize on where the market is and where it's going as easily. It can convey these competitive advantages because:

- The DMEDI approach provides a rich toolkit for focusing on the customer and understanding, synthesizing, and communicating customer needs. That means that customer needs and requirements are documented in a way that all participants can understand and refer to as needed throughout the project.

- It forces a level of deep discussion that leads to innovative approaches, in part because issues are viewed from all perspectives very early in the design process. The expectation is also established that multiple design alternatives will be considered, keeping the design space open longer and allowing for greater creativity.
- The DMEDI tools provide a map for structured communication that normally doesn't happen on design projects. They balance input from *all* perspectives, not just from people with more power or particular expertise. Everyone on the design team will see the impact of his work on the other pieces of the puzzle.

Because of these components, DfLSS projects are more likely to generate rapid results that delight customers, build momentum, and increase buy-in—and lead to more innovative products, services, and processes that can be implemented at lower cost.

13

The Healthcare Frontier

Making Progress
Despite the Challenges

WITH RANDY BOYD

Given all the pressures on healthcare organizations, it's not surprising that many healthcare practitioners are looking to Lean Six Sigma to help address industry challenges. Is this a good strategy? Some think that using improvement disciplines in healthcare is almost impossible because healthcare is simply too different—patients are not widgets, every situation is unique, the relationships between the many players are too complex, and so on.

Admittedly, there are obvious differences between healthcare and most other sectors—primarily because the lives and welfare of real people are put at risk every day. Anyone who works in the healthcare system knows there are other significant differences as well, including the incredible degree of complexity created when patient and provider needs collide with government, regulatory, and insurance requirements. In how many other industries do so many players compete for the same dollars? How many other industries have the potential to affect every single person?

Despite those factors, there are more similarities than differences between healthcare and other businesses—all entities need to procure and manage supplies, pay bills and wages, and manage diverse staffing demands. Any process within healthcare can be studied and improved, and many of them affect patient welfare. For example:

- A recent study released by Healthgrades showed that, based on a review of 37 million patient records, an average of 195,000 people in the United States die each year because of potentially preventable in-hospital medical errors.
- A Harvard University study for the state of New York suggests that 1.3 million people are injured each year in hospitals, and 118,000 of them will die from those injuries. Most of those injuries are preventable.

Wherever processes and process problems exist, Lean Six Sigma has a role to play. The methodology can help reduce waste and improve quality in healthcare just as it can in other industries. It can help reduce the unneeded complexity that plagues healthcare processes, and make it easier to deal with complexity that cannot be reduced. As just one example, the previous 20,000 or so international classification of disease (ICD) codes used to identify specific diseases and conditions has recently been replaced by more like 90,000 ICD codes.

In this chapter, we'll talk about the role for Lean Six Sigma in healthcare and discuss the deployment challenges and opportunities that healthcare organizations will face.

LEAN SIX SIGMA APPLICATIONS IN HEALTHCARE

Like every company, healthcare businesses do their work through processes. And any process can be studied and improved using basic Lean Six Sigma methods. Figure 13.1 shows a process view of a healthcare company, where the core value stream is built around having a patient arrive, receive treatment (or not), and then leave. The treatments vary, and how the entrance and exit take place will change from patient to patient and facility to facility, but the basic flow of entrance–treatment–exit is universal. As with any other business, if the core value stream of a healthcare organization is to function effectively, there have to be many support processes. These include the administrative functions that allow the hospital to run effectively and the supply chain operations that provide the needed supplies and equipment.

Most of the entrance, exit, and support processes are the same kind of transactional processes that occur in any business. Other processes are basically logistics—making sure that the right supplies, equipment, and medications are where they need to be, in the right quantity, and at the right time.

Once you start looking at these functions as processes, it becomes clear that there are many opportunities for applying Lean Six Sigma to make improvements. Example projects in each of these areas are shown in Table 13.1.

Lean Six Sigma has already been very successful in many healthcare organizations. For example, a hospital was averaging 90 minutes to complete the turnover of operating rooms used for hip and knee replacements. Using Lean tools—including value stream maps, waste assessments, 5S methods, and quick changeover—the hospital was able to reduce turnover to less than 30 minutes, saving

FIGURE **13.1** Healthcare core processes

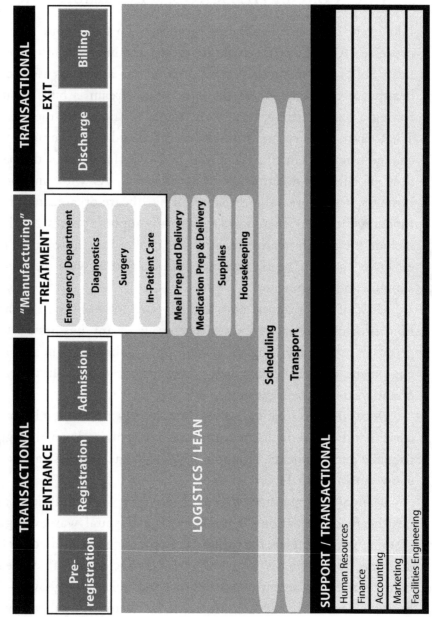

TABLE **13.1** Example LSS projects in healthcare

	Project Type	Key Relevant LSS Tools
Exit and Entry Transactional	*Cycle time:* • Registration • Admission • Discharge *Working capital:* • Reduce time between discharge and billing • Insurance coding accuracy *Quality:* • Improve customer satisfaction scores on admission or discharge • Improve medication tracking accuracy from admission to discharge	VOC—interviews and surveys Process mapping/VSM Setup reduction Process load balancing Statistical tools Mistake-proofing
Treatment	*Wait time:* • Reduce ER wait times • Reduce time from arrival to bed	Process mapping/VSM Simulation Statistical tools Root cause analysis tools Quick changeover FMEA
Logistics	*Inventory:* • Improve consumable replenishment process • Reduce cost of inventory on hand (pharma, ortho, endo, cardio) • Distribution and management of medications • Room turnover	Pull systems ABC stratification Batch size optimization Quick changeover

60 minutes in cycle time. That made the rooms available for additional operational procedures each day, meaning that more patients could receive treatment more quickly. In addition, the hospital replicated the ideas with similar procedures used in other surgeries, and saw gains in multiple areas.

Here is a sampling of other ways in which healthcare organizations have used Lean Six Sigma to create operational improvements:

- A healthcare provider system in New Jersey has had a vigorous Six Sigma program in place for several years as part of its initiative to achieve operational excellence. In one project focused on congestive heart failure, length of stay was reduced from 6 to 4 days, and chart consistency improved from 67 percent to 93 percent.
- A medical center in Connecticut achieved a 75 percent reduction in bloodstream infection rates in the surgical intensive care unit, with $1.2 million annually in estimated savings.
- One project at a university medical center's cath lab increased available capacity by 2.08 patients per lab per weekday, with a potential revenue impact of $5.2 million annually.
- A health system headquartered in Washington has been implementing Six Sigma and change management on an enterprisewide basis across four regions, and has a number of completed projects covering various operational and clinical issues. Total savings achieved so far exceeds $40 million.
- A specialty hospital in Rhode Island successfully used Six Sigma and change management to standardize operating procedures for embryo transfer, yielding a 35 percent increase in implantation rates.
- A hospital in Los Angeles reduced registry expenses by mapping multiple process drivers, achieving a cost savings of over $5 million.
- A clinic identified that it was losing thousands of dollars each month as a result of outdated medications and medical

supplies. Applying the Lean technique known as a "two-bin replenishment pull system" throughout the clinic allowed it to eliminate significant costs associated with outdated medications and medical supplies each month.

- A hospital in the southwestern United States had data showing that 13 percent of billings were being rejected by the insurance carriers because of incorrect demographics such as missing social security numbers, incorrect addresses, diagnosis codes not matching, and the like. Making improvements in its third-party billing system is saving the hospital $5 million per quarter.
- A veterans' hospital gained $42 million annually by improving the diagnosis coding of patient records.

REDUCING COMPLEXITY

In the world of quality improvement, complexity is an unparalleled source of waste, delays, and errors in processes. Some complexity in healthcare organizations is imposed from the outside by regulations, insurers, and government agencies, and there may not be much that they can do about that. But there is also a significant amount of complexity that is self-induced—and that can be addressed with Lean Six Sigma.

Healthcare organizations can be their own worst enemies in some ways, creating internal complexity that imposes enormous but underappreciated costs. One example is the standard practice of allowing clinics to act independently. When we visit a clinic, if we ask the staff members, "Who do you work for?" the answers are typically either "I work for this clinical area" or "I work for that doctor." People do *not* say, "I work for the XYZ Healthcare System." There is a mindset in many clinics and hospitals that allows clinical areas to behave as if they were private practices.

That independence and control sounds great from the viewpoint of the clinical specialties, but it's not good for the organization. These clinical areas tend to prioritize what is best for them individually, not what serves the organization overall. That level of independence would not be tolerated in other kinds of organizations; a bank, for example, would never consider allowing the tellers at each of its 5,600 branches to decide on their own way of conducting work!

Yet in healthcare, independence and control for each clinical area impose additional complexities on the organization as a result of these decisions. Each area will often expect to be able to customize *everything* about how its practice is run. For example, one clinic had 200 different consent forms because each clinical area felt that it had to add something specific to its version of the basic consent form. (The clinic later standardized on three consent forms, with additional specific information taken at the time of the patient's visit. This eliminated massive amounts of paperwork, reduced clinical editing errors, and simplified medical records management.)

Scheduling rules for appointments are another source of complexity in clinical settings. An appointment for a new patient, for example, needs to be longer so that there is additional time to assess the patient, get to know him, and find out pertinent information that will assist in future medical decisions. While a certain level of scheduling rule flexibility is necessary and understandable, a clinic with hundreds of physicians that allows each of them to have her own set of rules creates major headaches for schedulers. Imagine the workload this imposes on the staff member who is fielding a scheduling call from a patient. He has to wade through thousands of rules to figure out which ones apply to the particular physician and patient in question. If a patient cancels an appointment, it's very difficult for the clinic to find a replacement because of the strict requirements. Simply standardizing rules by clinical areas has brought huge dividends in terms of reducing both complexity and the time it takes to work through the scheduling process.

Some healthcare organizations operate with a physician- or specialty-centered mindset, and changing that focus will not be popular. But if you understand the costs that complexity imposes on a process, and the cumulative effect on the organization's efficiency and profitability, you will realize that the "private practice" approach, when implemented in a large healthcare system, imposes costs that no organization can support for any length of time. Your guide has to be what is best for both the patients and the business. Lean Six Sigma methodologies have the benefit of reducing organizational complexity, thus freeing up physicians and clinicians to spend more of their valuable time on patient care.

We are *not* advocating that all decision making be removed from the physician or clinical area's hands. That would be absurd. But the balance of control currently leans too far toward the individual practice in a clinical practice setting, and healthcare organizations must look for ways to reduce complexity, focus on the patient, improve medical outcomes, and be cost-competitive in today's market.

A much more efficient approach is to involve physicians and staff members in a discussion aimed at reaching consensus about the areas where autonomy helps them best serve the welfare of the patients. Then everything else—meaning processes and tasks that do not directly affect patient care—should be examined with a more holistic process mindset. Then make improvements accordingly, such as standardizing the scheduling processes and consent forms, as discussed earlier, and developing new standards for everything from requests for particular office supplies to improving the use of electronic medical records.

DEPLOYMENT CHALLENGES IN HEALTHCARE

When it comes to deployment strategies, there are more similarities than differences when comparing healthcare organizations to other businesses. The overall approach to deployment in healthcare will have the same components seen in any other organization, such as:

- Conducting an assessment up front to evaluate status and opportunities
- Mapping core value streams and identifying the performance measures that need to be improved
- Launch: training the resources and starting projects
- Maturity and sustainability: project monitoring, expansion, and integration into the organization

Yet as with the application of Lean Six Sigma methodologies, there are differences in the deployment details for healthcare organizations that have proved to be challenging if they are not addressed directly.

Challenge 1: Change Management

The people dimension of change and improvement is important in every organization, but it is critical to survival in healthcare deployments. The switch to becoming more process- and patient-focused is profound, and healthcare organizations that underestimate its impact have struggled to develop a successful, sustainable Lean Six Sigma deployment.

That's why healthcare organizations need to go the extra mile in their change management efforts if they want improvement methods to take root. Their deployment plans should address such issues as:

- *Making sure that the leaders are on board.* Leadership support is important in any broad initiative because efforts cannot be sustained unless the organization's leaders support the activities, both verbally and through their actions. The broader change management issues in healthcare make top leadership support even more critical.

- *Being careful about choosing the right people to fill the deployment positions.* These people will serve as the change agents. They must be persuasive and passionate. They don't need a background in statistics, but they should not be afraid of technical tools.
- *Taking extra steps to build a process focus throughout the organization.* All staff members should have the mindset that the work they do is accomplished through processes that can be improved.
- *Engaging physicians at every step.* The effort can start in support processes, but it will not survive in the long term if physicians are not on board.

One factor that works in your favor in terms of building a compelling argument concerning the need for process improvement is all the changes that are going on in the healthcare industry. In any organization, the reasons *for* change must overwhelm the *resistance* to change. Making that case in today's healthcare environment is relatively easy. Demand for services is rising, as are costs, and reimbursements are going down. In short, you have a sense of urgency and a compelling need for improvement on your side. You must work to communicate it.

Challenge 2: Developing Relevant, Engaging Training

Lean Six Sigma resources in healthcare come from a variety of backgrounds. Many will have extensive scientific backgrounds (and may be comfortable with statistics); others will not. To address this diversity, healthcare training in Lean Six Sigma should:

- Incorporate specific healthcare examples for every concept.
- Emphasize the right Lean and statistical tools to drive results.
- Focus on how to use the tools, but avoid detailed mathematical formulas.

Challenge 3: Accounting for Stakeholder Complexity

While the fundamentals of process improvement are the same no matter what the setting, projects in healthcare differ in the relationships between the steps and the players (see Figure 13.2). In healthcare processes, it's not always clear who the suppliers and customers are. For example, a hospital is a *supplier* to the patient but a *customer* of the physician. Similarly, an employee can be both a supplier and a customer in some processes. Plus, many processes will cross paths with many different stakeholders.

FIGURE **13.2** Complex relationships

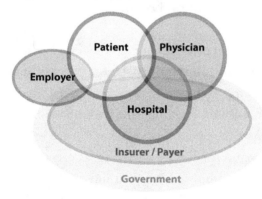

There are many overlapping and often conflicting relationships in healthcare that have to be considered. For example, if you focus solely on improving patient outcomes, you may have a negative impact on insurance agency outcomes. Though you may need to be more patient-focused, steps taken to improve a patient's experience could affect his physician. You cannot overemphasize stakeholder analysis tools when working in process improvement.

Challenge 4: Working with Physicians

Physicians control and/or influence many of the processes in a healthcare setting, and rightly so. That's why engaging physicians in the improvement effort right from the start is absolutely critical. The goal should be to involve them, educate them about Lean Six Sigma and how it has been used in healthcare companies, and work with them in focusing on the holistic process and how each subprocess affects the whole.

Share the data that show why change is needed. Emphasize the potential for improving patient outcomes and the impact both on them personally and on the business (such as reducing the amount of non-value-added work and documentation that physicians must complete for each patient).

Making time for physician involvement is always a challenge. Start small by finding one or two who will agree to serve as advisors on pilot projects that will free up *their* time for more patient care. That could include tackling issues such as reducing the number of administrative tasks and/or making those tasks simpler—or any kind of project that will make their lives easier. Once physicians see the results and feel the impact of quality improvement efforts, they often become enthusiastic supporters.

Controlling the Controllable

There are many issues in the healthcare sector that are not under the control of providers, some of which are subject to change depending on political and societal forces. Providers also have much more complex stakeholder relationships than most other businesses. But in what may feel like a dark tunnel, Lean Six Sigma methods offer a glimmer of light. They help providers better control the aspects of their operations that are within their span of influence.

So while a provider may not be able to reduce the number of medical codes imposed by the government, she *can* create processes that are able to deal with that complexity with minimal cost and stress to her business systems. While she cannot control what kinds of reimbursements government agencies and insurers will make, she *can* create internal efficiencies that will allow her to provide better care to more patients at a lower cost.

This ability to control the controllable is why we view Lean Six Sigma as a vital competitive element for healthcare organizations. Improving processes and systems lets them create a more resilient and flexible organization that can respond quickly, even in an unpredictable environment like healthcare.

Appendix A

A Complete
Maturity Model

As discussed in Chapter 6, a maturity model is a framework that helps companies in three ways:

1. Understanding how deployments typically evolve
2. Evaluating the current status of a deployment
3. Setting targets for improvement

A typical maturity model describes various components of a deployment and different levels of success or maturity for each component. Our model includes the five components that have the biggest influence over the future of a deployment:

1. Strategy
2. Projects
3. Resources
4. Training
5. Culture

For each component, we have described five levels of progression, starting with Introductory and ending with Setting the Standard. The following five tables show the factors that we've found most critical in each component and the success levels for that factor.

TABLE A.1 Strategy section of the maturity model

Strategy		Level 1 Introductory	Level 2 Initial Results	Level 3 Demonstrating Success	Level 4 Successful, Mature Deployment	Level 5 Setting the Standard
1	Deployment alignment with business strategy	Not considered	Lean Six Sigma is considered to be a robust problem-solving methodology	Some consider Lean Six Sigma to be a key methodology for execution of the corporate strategy	Leaders consider Lean Six Sigma to be a key methodology for execution of the corporate strategy	Lean Six Sigma is culturally the way things are done, and integrally aligned with the execution of the corporate strategy
2	Project alignment with business strategy	Projects chosen for convenience	Projects chosen opportunistically, bottom-up	Projects align well with business priorities in some areas	Most projects align with business priorities and metrics	Linkage and traceability from project metrics to key strategic metrics
3	Breadth of deployment	Single functional area or single geography	More than one functional area or geography	Deployment across all manufacturing and service areas, some transactional; multiple geographies	Deployment expands to transactional processes and supporting functions across multiple geographies	All functional areas, including R&D, sales, and shared services. All geographies

#					
4	None identified	Deployment managed by a Black belt practitioner	Deployment led by a representative from middle management	Deployment led by a representative from the executive team, reporting to VP level	Deployment led by a representative from the executive team, reporting to C level
	Deployment leader				
5	None identified	Deployment driven by a representative from middle management	Deployment driven by VP level, direct report to executive team	Deployment driven by a representative from the executive team, such as the COO or CFO	Deployment is CEO-driven
	Overall deployment executive sponsorship				
6	None identified	Breakeven	5X	10X	20X
	Total return on investment (long-term deployment)				
7	Project-level metrics exist	Project-level metrics exist, with some tracking of the overall program	Deployment-wide metrics exist	Deployment-wide metrics exist, including financial impact on both the income statement and the balance sheet, along with project cycle times	Lean Six Sigma metrics are integrated with corporate dashboards
	Metrics				

(continued)

TABLE A.1 Strategy section of the maturity model (*continued*)

Strategy	Level 1 Introductory	Level 2 Initial Results	Level 3 Demonstrating Success	Level 4 Successful, Mature Deployment	Level 5 Setting the Standard
8	Finance participation	No significant involvement from finance	Finance involved on an ad hoc basis when requested	Finance representatives identified, trained, and participating on a significant number of project teams	Finance fully engaged, establishing, training, and auditing financial guidelines	Finance assists the business units in linking project benefits directly to budget review and planning
9	Linkage to performance planning	None	Lean Six Sigma linked to performance planning for the belt	Lean Six Sigma linked to performance planning for the belts, teams, and sponsors	Continuous improvement linked to performance planning for all employees	Continuous improvement fully integrated into the culture. No longer needed beyond the belts, teams, and sponsors

TABLE A.2   Projects section of the maturity model

Projects		Level 1 Introductory	Level 2 Initial Results	Level 3 Demonstrating Success	Level 4 Successful, Mature Deployment	Level 5 Setting the Standard
1	Overall results	Nothing significant	Some good results at the project level	Most projects have significant, measurable impact	The projects in aggregate make a significant impact on key business metrics	Significant driver of value for the business, worthy of mention in the annual report
2	Financial results per Black belt project	Not calculated	Averaging more than $100,000 per Black belt project (large company)	Averaging more than $200,000 per Black belt project (large company)	Averaging more than $300,000 per Black belt project (large company)	Averaging more than $400,000 per Black belt project (large company)
3	Financial results per Green belt project	Not calculated	Averaging more than $25,000 per Green belt project (large company)	Averaging more than $50,000 per Green belt project (large company)	Averaging more than $75,000 per Green belt project (large company)	Averaging more than $100,000 per Green belt project (large company)
4	Cycle times per Black belt project	Not calculated	Averaging more than a year	Averaging 9–12 months per project	Averaging 7–8 months per project, depending on project scope	Averaging 6 months or less per project, depending on project scope

(continued)

TABLE A.2 Projects section of the maturity model (*continued*)

Projects		Level 1 Introductory	Level 2 Initial Results	Level 3 Demonstrating Success	Level 4 Successful, Mature Deployment	Level 5 Setting the Standard
5	Cycle times per Green belt project	Not calculated	Averaging 10+ months	Averaging 6–9 months per project	Averaging 4–5 months per project, depending on project scope	Averaging 3 months or less per project, depending on project scope
6	Project selection and prioritization methodology	None	Projects are selected and prioritized based on a discussion with the manager. No official processes	Official project selection methodology is implemented in some parts of the business. Projects are prioritized and actively managed	Robust project selection methodology is broadly implemented and clearly linked to business strategy	Robust assessment-based project selection methodology, clearly linked to business strategy. Projects are prioritized across the business

#					
7	No clear output metric identified	Projects use a few basic tools, but no statistics	Output metrics and input metrics identified. Good tool use on the easier tools. Missed opportunities to apply tools that would be relevant and valuable	Broad understanding of the benefits of the more rigorous tools. Most of the relevant tools are utilized	Projects take advantage of all relevant tools. The tools illustrate the impact that the project had on the key metric, graphically and statistically
	Tool rigor				
8	Weak Control phase. No interest beyond the Black belt	Consistent effort made by Black belt to track, control, and sustain project results	Process owners identified, but some handoff issues exist. Implementation plans exist, but some are not fully implemented	Solid control plans. Mostly smooth transitions to process owners. Stated benefits are monitored and reported in a Validate gate	Significant project metrics are visibly and easily tracked by process owners, including leveraging statistical analysis. Stated benefits are successfully validated
	Control and sustainment				

(continued)

TABLE A.2 Projects section of the maturity model (*continued*)

Projects		Level 1 Introductory	Level 2 Initial Results	Level 3 Demonstrating Success	Level 4 Successful, Mature Deployment	Level 5 Setting the Standard
9	Replication	None	Some replication attempted	A process exists to identify and execute replication projects	A process exists to identify and execute replication projects, and there have been significant successes	Replication opportunities are routinely identified and successfully implemented
10	Project tracking	None	Initial spreadsheet	Tracking information is rolled up across the deployment	Internally developed tracking database	Central database with tracking and approval work flows

TABLE A.3 Resources section of the maturity model

Resources		Level 1 Introductory	Level 2 Initial Results	Level 3 Demonstrating Success	Level 4 Successful, Mature Deployment	Level 5 Setting the Standard
1	Quality of talent	Some involuntary selection	Participation is driven by personal interest and availability	There is a formal people-selection process	There is a formal people-selection process that ensures strong candidates in Black belt, Master Black belt, and champion roles	Deployment has a demonstrated track record of current and future business leaders in Black belt, Master Black belt, and champion roles
2	Repatriation	No plan	Former full-time belt returns to old job	Some Black belts are promoted after the Black belt commitment. General consensus that the experience has provided opportunities for skill development	Some Black belts are promoted after the Black belt commitment. General consensus that the experience has provided increased likelihood of future professional advancement	Significant percentage of Black belts are promoted after Black belt commitment has been successfully completed

(continued)

TABLE A.3 Resources section of the maturity model (*continued*)

Resources		Level 1 Introductory	Level 2 Initial Results	Level 3 Demonstrating Success	Level 4 Successful, Mature Deployment	Level 5 Setting the Standard
3	Alumni	New program—no alumni	Alumni experience as Black belt highly variable, with some openly negative	Alumni generally had a positive experience, but little or no ongoing engagement	Alumni continue to be engaged and supportive of the program	Alumni are a significant driver of the culture of continuous improvement. Alumni demonstrate the desired Lean Six Sigma characteristics after repatriation
4	Recognition	None	Acknowledgment of training through certificate	Acknowledgment of certification through certificate, plaque, or commemorative item. Recognition is communicated throughout the organization	Multiple modes of recognition, appropriate to level of project success. Recognition is provided to the team, not just the belt	Systematic rewards and recognition program, including certification, project recognition, and team recognition

TABLE A.4 Training section of the maturity model

Training		Level 1 Introductory	Level 2 Initial Results	Level 3 Demonstrating Success	Level 4 Successful, Mature Deployment	Level 5 Setting the Standard
1	Training methodology	Training is provided on a continuous improvement methodology, usually by outside consultants or universities	Training is provided in Lean Six Sigma, usually by outside consultants or universities	Training is provided in Lean Six Sigma, kaizen, and Design for Lean Six Sigma	Organization has full capability to deliver Lean Six Sigma training internally, including product and process Design for Lean Six Sigma	Organization has full capability to deliver training internally, including ongoing Master Black belt–level training
2	Breadth of training	Project leaders self-study	Training is provided to project leaders	Training is provided to project leaders, champions, and sponsors	Training is provided to project leaders, champions, and sponsors; 80% of sponsors are trained prior to project start	Training is provided to project leaders, champions, and sponsors; all sponsors are trained prior to project start. Most of the company has attended awareness training

(continued)

TABLE A.4 Training section of the maturity model (*continued*)

Training	Level 1 Introductory	Level 2 Initial Results	Level 3 Demonstrating Success	Level 4 Successful, Mature Deployment	Level 5 Setting the Standard
3	Project coaching (Black belt)	None	A coach is identified, but his qualifications only slightly exceed those of the belt being coached, or he has very limited availability	A qualified coach is identified, with sufficient capacity to meet with the Black belt on a regular basis to coach his first project	Certified Master Black belts are providing the Black belt coaching, and they have sufficient capacity to meet with the Black belt on a regular basis to coach his first project	Certified Master Black belts are providing coaching on a regular basis for all new Black belt projects, as well as supporting additional projects that are challenging, and offering remedial help as needed

TABLE A.5 Culture section of the maturity model

Culture		Level 1 Introductory	Level 2 Initial Results	Level 3 Demonstrating Success	Level 4 Successful, Mature Deployment	Level 5 Setting the Standard
1	Lean Six Sigma engagement	Primary engagement is at the individual level	Primary engagement is at the project-team level	In addition to engagement of the project teams, there is a broad awareness across the business	In addition to engagement of the project teams, there is a broad awareness across the business, and significant pull for project teams	Lean Six Sigma is integral to the culture of the business. There is nearly 100% awareness and strong favorable opinion of the program
2	Continuous improvement mindset	Mindset that continuous improvement is not needed	Continuous improvement program is in place, but is perceived as extra work, with key pockets of resistance	Solid continuous improvement program is in place	Successful continuous improvement program is in place, with strong favorable opinion	Strong continuous improvement culture. People across the business are looking at all key processes for ongoing improvement opportunities

(continued)

TABLE A.5 Culture section of the maturity model (*continued*)

Culture		Level 1	Level 2	Level 3	Level 4	Level 5
		Introductory	Initial Results	Demonstrating Success	Successful, Mature Deployment	Setting the Standard
3	Customer-centric	Not customer-focused	No official voice of the customer processes	Voice of the customer gathered within specific Lean Six Sigma projects, but not applied more broadly to key business decisions	Some areas of the business have established voice of the customer processes, and are heavily focused on meeting customer needs. Gaps exist in other business areas	Broad understanding of customer requirements at every level in the company. Key decisions are made from the perspective of how they will help the customer
4	Process-centric	No effort to understand businesswide value streams	Value streams not well understood. No end-to-end process ownership	Value streams are well understood, but without end-to-end process ownership	Value stream management in place with appropriate process ownership	Value stream management in place with appropriate process ownership. Processes have strategic targets
5	Data-centric	Data are not available for key business decisions	Key business decisions are based mostly on intuition and experience	Some areas are heavily data-driven in their decision making; other areas primarily use intuition	Key business decisions are based on data. Some processes are managed with process control	Key business decisions are based on statistically driven data. Most core processes are managed with process control

Index

Pages number followed by f, t, indicate figures, tables respectively.

About the Authors

Kimberly Watson-Hemphill is the president and CEO of Firefly Consulting, a company she founded in 2009. She is a globally known expert in the field of innovation and operational excellence, and is a coauthor of *Fast Innovation* (McGraw-Hill, 2005). Kimberly has led Lean Six Sigma programs in multiple manufacturing and service industries, including a deployment with a global Fortune 500 company that generated more than $1 billion in savings. She was previously a partner with Accenture and a vice president of George Group Consulting, and is currently on the faculty of the Acton School of Business. Her educational background includes a BSE in aerospace engineering and a BA in French from the University of Michigan, as well as an MSE in engineering mechanics from the University of Texas. She is a certified Master Black Belt.

Kristine Nissen Bradley is a principal with Firefly Consulting. She is a certified Master Black Belt in both Lean Six Sigma and Design for Lean Six Sigma, and has worked with thousands of business leaders and practitioners to successfully deploy these methodologies over the last 25 years. She has implemented process improvement methods for clients around the world, with an emphasis on driving organic internalization of these techniques. Kristine completed an MBA from Duke University Fuqua School of Business and was named a Fuqua Scholar. She also received an MS in mechanical engineering from Texas A&M University and a BS in industrial engineering from Texas A&M University.

CPSIA information can be obtained
at www.ICGtesting.com
Printed in the USA
BVHW042211131119
563642BV00017B/78/P

9 781259 584404